Thi
Bel

PRIMROSES and CATKINS © Gay Corran 1986

AYR STORIES

AYR STORIES

Dane Love

FORT PUBLISHING

First published in 2000 by Fort Publishing Ltd, Old Belmont House,
12 Robsland Avenue, Ayr, KA7 2RW.

Designed by Paul McLaughlin, 48 Queen Street, Lochmaben, DG11 1PS

Printed by Bell and Bain Ltd., Glasgow

Typeset in 10.5pt Sabon by Senga Fairgrieve, 0131 658 1763

ISBN 0-9536576-1-2

A catalogue record for this book is available from the British Library

CONTENTS

List of Illustrations

Acknowledgements

The author would like to thank a few people for their assistance in the preparation of this book. They are Roger Clark, Hugh Robertson, John Thomson, Gordon Irving, Ronald Brash, John Dalton and, of course, the ever-helpful staff of the Carnegie Library, without whom no book on Ayr could ever be written.

INTRODUCTION

AYR IS ONE OF the oldest towns in Scotland. It has a fascinating past and almost every significant period in Scottish history has been mirrored in the Auld Toon, from the Wars of Independence to the Covenanters and the Suffragette campaigns. For centuries it was more important in strategic and commercial terms than Glasgow; in fact, the first parliament after the battle of Bannockburn in 1314 was convened twelve months later in the Church of St John in Ayr. Its long and turbulent history has thrown up a wealth of dramatic events, tales and colourful characters. For the historian and storyteller, there is a veritable embarrassment of riches.

The origins of Ayr as a settlement are something of a mystery. It is thought the area was populated during the Mesolithic period (12000 to 3000 BC) but the evidence is sketchy and inconclusive. However, recent archaeological finds have revealed that the area had a significant population during the Bronze Age (between 2000 and 500 BC). It is also speculated that Ayr was occupied by the Romans, but again hard facts are in short supply. Proof positive of events during the Dark Ages is equally hard to come by, although it is clear that waves of immigrants arrived at regular intervals.

The first written evidence available to historians dates from 1197 when William the Lion, King of Scots, built a royal castle between the Rivers Ayr and Doon. It became known as Newcastle-upon-Ayr and a small settlement grew up in the castle's environs. Eight years later, in 1205, William created the burgh of Ayr when he granted a royal charter. From this time, Ayr grew and prospered, with its economy greatly assisted by the town's position at the mouth of the River Ayr.

The stories in this book reflect the town's history, economy and politics from that time. Inevitably, there has been much conflict. There are Wallace's battles with the English on the streets of

Ayr, and Oliver Cromwell's decision to make it the biggest of the five forts he built to control the Scots. The deadly blood feud of the Kennedys, a family that dominated this part of Ayrshire for centuries, is given due prominence. The good citizens of seventeenth-century Ayr were strongly committed to the Covenanting cause and the chapter on this theme describes yet more conflict and bloodshed.

However, there is much more to Ayr's history than warfare and the breadth of subjects in this book is testament to that fact. For centuries, women suspected of being witches were harshly treated throughout Scotland, and Ayr was no exception to the rule. Smuggling was a national problem and once again Ayr was to the fore. As a leading commercial centre, it would be remiss of the local historian to overlook the Ayr Bank crash of 1772, Ayr as a centre of shipbuilding and the town's important role in the development of modern roadmaking.

Ayr has many notable landmarks and features, each with their own tale to tell. The much loved Low Green has a long history and has been used for many purposes including football, croquet, open-air entertainment, as a meeting place and even as an airfield. The brigs of Ayr are known throughout the world, immortalised in the eponymous poem by Robert Burns. The Auld Kirk of St John is another institution with an interesting past, not least in the frequent incursions by body snatchers desperate to spirit away fresh corpses to hospitals in Glasgow and Edinburgh.

Given the importance of Ayr to life in Scotland, it would be surprising if it was not associated with people pre-eminent in their own fields. The most famous by some distance is of course the Bard, Robert Burns, who was born in Alloway, educated in Ayr and drew much of his inspiration from the Auld Toon and its citizens. There is also David Cathcart who rose to prominence as a judge in the Court of Session and took the title Lord Alloway in the process. The story of an outsider who became a resident is also recounted: the iron and steel tycoon James Baird was one of the most remarkable men of the Victorian age. And no book on Ayr would be complete without mention of that kenspeckle character, John Miller, otherwise known as Baron Miller.

Ayr has not been exempt from the political upheavals of the last century and this aspect of its history is well covered in the book. One of the most dramatic events was the Radical uprising of 1820, an event that sent shockwaves through the Scottish political establishment, and saw soldiers on the streets of Ayr. An equally momentous campaign occurred almost a century later as the women of Britain fought for universal suffrage. In Ayr, as in other parts of the country the campaign was bitter, hard fought and at times violent.

The modern period is also well represented. Ayr's much loved tram system opened for business in 1901 and was an invaluable asset for the town until its closure in 1931. There is the story of the Popplewell family and the Gaiety Theatre which, of course, still flourishes today. A chapter is devoted to Ayr in the Second World War, while Ayr's importance as a holiday resort is considered in *Doon the Watter*. Politics too makes an appearance: *Father of the Commons* looks at the colourful career of Sir Thomas Moore, MP, who represented the Ayr constituency for nearly forty years.

Nor is sport neglected. Horse-racing has a long and distinguished lineage in Ayr and the town is now Scotland's leading venue; no look at Ayr would be complete without it. Another institution close to people's hearts is Ayr United FC, a team with a proud past and ambitious plans for the future. The book closes with an account of one of the most dramatic cases in Scottish criminal history: the wrongful conviction of Paddy Meehan for the murder of a wealthy Ayr resident.

Despite the range of subjects covered in these twenty-six stories there are many more which need to be told. There is, for example, the large group of ancient buildings which have been lost to the town including Ayr Castle, St Leonard's Chapel (today the site of the Wallace Tower), Newton Castle and the two monasteries of Blackfriars and Greyfriars. The redevelopment of major parts of the town in recent years has also been significant: for example the relocation of Ayr Harbour and the demolition of Ayr County Hospital. Many other eminent people hailed from Ayr, or became associated with it through residence: the former group includes

Johannes Scotus Erigena, the ninth-century philosopher, Andrew Michael Ramsay, tutor to Bonnie Prince Charlie and better known as Chevalier de Ramsay, and England cricket captain Mike Denness. While the latter encompasses Sir William Arrol, the great civil engineer responsible for designing the Forth Road Bridge and the second Tay Bridge. All in all, we have excellent foundations for a second book of *Ayr Stories*!

Dane Love
Auchinleck,
July 2000.

I
WALLACE HASTES TO AYR

THE GREAT SCOTS freedom fighter William Wallace had many close links with Auld Ayr. Ayrshire folk claim that he was born at Ellerslie, which was owned by his father Sir Malcolm Wallace, on the outskirts of Kilmarnock. His uncle, Sir Adam Wallace, was the proprietor of Riccarton Castle, the site of which is now occupied by Kilmarnock fire station, where an appropriate commemorative plaque has been mounted.

Blind Harry the Minstrel, writing in the fifteenth century, records that Wallace killed an English soldier at the cross of Ayr. This probably took place at the site of the Malt Cross, where the High Street joins the Sandgate. Tradition claims that the English soldier was inviting passers-by to try and attack him with his staff, offering them a prize of one groat if they were successful. No one was willing to try until Wallace came forward. As Blind Harry records:

> Which story when it came to Wallace' ear,
> To smile and laugh, he scarce could well forbear:
> He told the fellow that he would be willing,
> For one Scots blow, to give an English shilling.
> The greedy wretch did freely condescend,
> Which quickly brought him to his fatal end:
> When Wallace gave him such a dreadful thump,
> Upon his back, close by his great fat rump,
> That to the view of all were present there,
> He clave his rig bone, and ne'er spake mair.
> Thus died the wretch, for a poor price and small,
> And his great English hurdies paid for them all.

English soldiers were quickly on the scene, and Wallace was forced to defend himself. He struck one of the soldiers with the staff, 'till brains and bones did flee'. Others were killed by his sword, until:

> Five South'rons he, 'twixt hope and great despair,
> Kill'd on the spot; now was not that right fair?
> Out through the town, his way did cleanly force,
> Made his escape, and then did mount his horse:
> To Laiglands fled, his time well did use,
> And left the blades all sleeping in their shoes.

The escape route followed by Wallace was by way of the High Street and along the southern bank of the River Ayr. On the bank opposite Craigie House is a spot known as Wallace's Heel. According to local legend, some English soldiers were pursuing Wallace after he had slain their comrades at the cross. Wallace ran as fast as his massive frame could carry him. By the side of the river he dropped down to the waterside, where there were some slabs of rock. As he jumped from them as far into the river as he was able, his heel is said to have caused an indentation in the stone that gave the spot its name. Wallace's horse was tethered on the opposite side of the river, and on it he made his escape towards Auchincruive. Fresh water issued thereafter from a hole near the mark and the spot became a popular attraction. A metal ladle, chained to the rock, was once kept there to allow visitors to drink the water more comfortably. The site of the spring can be found by the riverside, near an old limekiln on the River Ayr walk.

In Leglen (or Laiglands) Wood stands a sizeable cairn that was erected in 1929 in memory of William Wallace and Robert Burns. This is located in Auchincruive estate, which in Wallace's day was owned by a distant kinsman. (The Wallaces retained ownership until about 1384.)

From the cairn, which is sited near Oswald's Bridge, a footpath through the wood leads to Wallace's Seat, one of a number of places associated with him on the banks of the River Ayr. Tradition states that the hero sat on this high promontory as he contemplated the bloody battles in front of him. Robert Burns visited the glen as a youth, walking from Mount Oliphant farm. He was aware of the patriot's association with the glen, and treated the walk as a form of pilgrimage. In a letter written on 15 November 1786, when he was twenty-six years old, he told Mrs Frances Anna Dunlop of Dunlop (whose maiden name was Wallace and who claimed the great patriot as an ancestor) of his journey:

> I chose a fine summer Sunday, the only day of the week in my power and walked half a dozen miles to pay my respects to the 'Leglen wood', with as much devout enthusiasm as ever Pilgrim did to Loretto; and as I explored every den and dell where I could suppose my heroic Countryman to have sheltered, I recollect (for even then I was a Rhymer) that my heart glowed with a wish to be able to make a Song on him equal to his merits.

On another occasion Wallace was sent by his uncle, Sir Reginald Craufurd, Sheriff of Ayr, to the Fish Cross to buy some fish. On his way back the steward of Lord Percy, the leader of the English garrison, stopped him and asked him to hand over the fish. Wallace, quite understandably, thought this unreasonable and a scuffle ensued in which Wallace drew his dagger and killed the steward. Soon eighty English soldiers surrounded Wallace and he was captured. He was taken to the tolbooth and incarcerated in the dungeon, where he was fed on nothing but herrings and water, causing him to weaken considerably. Indeed, so weak did his body become that his captors thought he was dead. They dragged his body from the tolbooth and threw it over the wall into a garden. Wallace's childhood nurse heard of this, and ran quickly to his side. Finding the slight traces of a pulse she managed to nurse him back to full strength.

A statue of Wallace is located on the first-floor wall of a building at the corner of Newmarket and High Streets. The building, dating from 1886, occupies the site of the tolbooth where Wallace was imprisoned. This is at least the second statue to occupy the site, for a previous structure erected by Henry Cowan in 1810 replaced a building that had a wooden effigy of Wallace on the wall. When the statue is viewed from the ground the legs look shorter than the rest of the body, and local legend has it that the sculptor had to rework them to fit the niche.

Another story from Blind Harry claims that Wallace came to Ayr in disguise, for he 'sorely long'd the town of Ayr to see'. At the burgh gate he spotted an English fencer who was taking part in a weapon show. The fencer asked the disguised hero if he would like to join in, to which Wallace responded in the affirmative, so long as the Englishman fenced with him. Naturally, his opponent was defeated and slain, whereupon a number of reinforcements appeared. Wallace killed twenty-nine 'South'ron men' in that affray before escaping once more to Leglen Wood.

The most famous tale linking Wallace with Ayr is that concerning the burning of the barns, the buildings where the burgh stored its grain. The traditional tale is rather gorier than the one generally accepted by historians, but many people find it wholly believable. According to Blind Harry's *Wallace*, a Court of Judiciary was proposed for the middle of the summer of 1299, which the English barons who ruled the country were expected to attend. Wallace and his men heard of this proposal and saw it as an ideal opportunity to settle their differences by peaceful means. And so he gathered together a number of local knights and they set out for the barns, where the court was to meet.

On the march towards Ayr, Sir Reginald Craufurd realised that he had forgotten to bring certain important legal documents with him. Wallace volunteered to hurry back to his castle to fetch them, intending to join the knights later. The knights, however, were quicker in reaching the town than was expected. At the barns they were invited in one by one. Instead of being engaged in debate as expected, the Scots knights were captured individually, and then hanged by the neck from the beams of the barn. According to tradition, those who suffered at the hands of the English included Sir Reginald, Bryce Blair of that Ilk, Sir Neil Montgomerie, Kennedy of Carrick, Barclay of Ardrossan and Boyd of Kilmarnock.

Word reached Wallace that the venture had gone horribly wrong. He then gathered together a force of supporters and waited until nightfall. In the summer gloaming the English feasted on a large banquet, delighted at their success in killing what they regarded as so many troublesome men. Wallace's men surrounded the barns, listening to the sound of merrymaking within. They gathered straw and hay and piled it around the building, and set it alight. Soon the building was ablaze, smoke spiralling into the darkened sky.

Inside the barns the drunken English soldiers took a while to realise that something was amiss. The dense smoke that bellowed from the straw asphyxiated many of them. Others nearer the doors ran as fast as they could into the streets, only to be met by Wallace's men. Their eyes streaming from the smoke, the English were unable to get clear sight of the Scots, who proceeded to run them through.

A second group of English soldiers, perhaps officers who wished a more comfortable bed, was billeted in the Blackfriars monastery (located in Mill Street, where Boots the Chemist now stands). They were lodged with a friar named Drumlaw. When the monks heard of Wallace's victory over the soldiers in the barns, they made their way to the dormitory and managed to kill the soldiers there, who had been disarmed on their arrival at the monastery. This act later became known as 'The Friars' Blessing'. The friars then joined Wallace's men who were systematically killing the English soldiers asleep in houses throughout the town. A female accomplice had gone beforehand, marking a chalk cross on the door of each dwelling where the enemy resided.

When the deed was done, Wallace and his men made a quick getaway. They headed to the north-east, climbing to the top of an eminence from where they could look back through the night sky towards Ayr. The flames were still leaping into the air, burning the last beams from the collapsed roof. As he gazed at the inferno, Wallace is said to have remarked, 'The barns o' Ayr burn weel.' From this saying the hill was known thereafter as Barnweill Hill.

Blind Harry states that five thousand English soldiers were killed that night. However, this assertion, like so many of the other claims in traditional accounts, must be viewed with a high degree of scepticism. Sir Reginald Craufurd was indeed executed by the English, but this took place at a later date, in February 1307. The execution is verified in reliable historical records as having taken place at Carlisle. There is more to connect Bryce Blair with Ayr. He was executed in a barn or barrack at Ayr, but this took place in the winter of 1306-7.

The burning of Ayr perhaps refers to the old castle, which was engulfed by fire on 19 August 1299. It was destroyed by the Scots to prevent it from falling into English hands. At the same time the town's barns may have been set alight, again to prevent them from being of any use to the advancing enemy. The location of the barns has been the subject of much speculation. Most accounts claim that they stood in what is now Mill Street, 'between the mill and Mill Lane, near where the Moravian Church now stands', according to an 1874 guide. Another account from 1847 claims that they stood near the Laigh Tolbooth, and that Henry Cowan erected a house on the site in 1810.

On another occasion, when the hero was slaying some English soldiers who had quartered themselves on the residents of the town, he was cornered on the first floor of a house in the High Street, near where the present Wallace Tower stands, but on the opposite side of the street. To escape capture by the pursuing soldiers he was able to exit by a window, landing in the street below. For many years a raised cobble in the High Street marked the spot where he landed. This was located in front of number 181, a building that was known as Wallace's Window.

Two surviving memorials in Ayr commemorate William Wallace. One of these is located at the Isle in the High Street, and has already been mentioned. The other is the better known of the two, and is located on the Wallace Tower, which stands in the High Street. The tower dates from 1834, when it was erected to the plans of Thomas Hamilton at a cost of £2,200. On a niche overlooking the High Street is a statue of the freedom fighter, carved by James Thom. It depicts the hero dressed in the armour of a classical hero, rather than the garb he would have worn. David Auld sponsored the sculptor and a public subscription paid for the remainder. The Wallace Tower occupies the site of a much older tower, which latterly was known as the Wallace Tower, but which in earlier times was referred to simply as the Old Tower. It was named the Wallace Tower not in honour of the hero but after the Wallaces of Craigie, who owned it for a time.

On Barnweill Hill a memorial tower was erected in memory of Wallace. This was paid for by William Patrick of Roughwood, near Beith, and built on land gifted by Brigadier-General James George Smith Neill of Barnweill and Swindridgemuir, whose statue is in Wellington Square. The tower was erected in 1856, and the architect and builder was R. Snodgrass of Beith. Within the tower a spiralling cantilever stairway climbs to a viewing platform on the roof, from where panoramic views can be enjoyed. These include the Galloway hills, Arran, Cairn Table, Ben Lomond, and even the Paps of Jura on a clear day. In 1898 the trustees passed the tower to the safekeeping of Ayr Common Good Fund. At one time a cottage stood at the foot of the tower, where a caretaker lived and welcomed visitors. Today the visitor requires to obtain the key of the door in Ayr.

To the south of Ayr, on the farm of Blairston Mains, is Wallace's Stone. A massive boulder, it measures over six feet by three feet, and is approximately two feet in height. According to tradition, Wallace laid his sword on the boulder for a short time. As it lay on the massive granitic stone some of his adherents marked around it with another rock, inscribing the shape of the great freedom fighter's weapon. The outline of the sword was later deepened, to become a permanent reminder of the hero's time there. The sword, which measures three and a half feet in length and fourteen inches across the hilt, is placed off-centre. The head of the sword is actually more like three arms of a Maltese cross. It is also true to say that the stone is probably earlier than Wallace's time, and would originally have stood erect. The 'sword' would then be a Christian cross, perhaps acting as a marker on the route taken by pilgrims. The stone was originally located in the Long Glen, half a mile south-west of its present position. In that glen, near the waterfall at the Halfway Bridge, was a Wallace Cave, but all traces of this seem to be lost. Six Clydesdale horses are said to have been needed to drag the stone to where it now lies, and it is said that it was proposed to move it to a more prominent location but that the men were unable to lift it. Instead, a stone wall was erected around it.

There are other theories associated with the stone. One claims that it commemorates a treaty of peace between the Scots and the Picts. J. Kevan McDowall, in his book *Carrick Gallovidian*, states that the name Wallace Stone is a corruption of the Gaelic *Uath al Aos Stadhaidhean*, meaning 'the solitary stone of age by the river winding'. Although this is perhaps an accurate description of its location, it can be dismissed as fanciful etymologising on McDowall's part!

2
THE LOW GREEN

TO LOCAL RESIDENTS THE Low Green is one of the town's most attractive and best-loved features. To visitors it is the enduring symbol of Ayr – the veritable jewel in the crown. Enjoyed the whole year round, it is especially busy in the summer months and remains a delight to all those who come in contact with it. But it also has a history full of surprises. That it has survived is one of them.

The Low Green is all that remains of the burgh's Common Lands still freely open to residents. A Royal Charter granted the Common to the burgh in the fourteenth century. Originally the Common occupied most of the parish, but over the centuries it was taken over and feued out to different people and organisations. The old racecourse was one of the last major losses, sixty-three acres being removed in 1770. According to the *New Statistical Account*:

> When or how the burgesses came to lose their right of *common-age* cannot well be ascertained. It must have been within the last forty years [i.e. 1797-1837], as it is stated to have been a common at the date of the last *Statistical Account* of Ayr; and its having ceased to be so, must doubtless have been with the consent, expressed or implied, of those having right to it.

The Low Green was used in the sixteenth century for 'the pastyme of the honest men in gayming according to use and wont'. Sports and games were played there throughout the succeeding centuries too. In 1870 part of the Green was laid out to allow women to play croquet. Ayr Thistle Football Club used other parts of the Green from 1872 until 1875. It was reported in 1872 that their pitch was much larger than was normal at the time. Ayr

Academy Football Club also played there between 1872 and 1876. Both teams had to find a new home pitch following a decision by the Council to prohibit football matches being played there due to the damage being caused to the turf.

Ayr Council began to recognise the potential for attracting tourists in the middle of the nineteenth century. The Low Green was seen as one of the town's main assets, and improvements were made to it in the 1880s. Up to this time the Green had been little more than grass-covered sand dunes, and these had to be flattened out. To carry out the work, men laid off due to a downturn in the carpet and weaving trade were taken on, and a fund was raised to pay them, this doubling as an act of relief. In 1881 the first stretch of the Esplanade was created when the sea wall was built. The wall was washed away the year after, but rebuilt. Extensions to it were made in 1893, until it eventually reached the mouth of the Doon. Park benches were erected at various points on the Green, as well as further south on the Esplanade, and a tall flagpole was raised at the Green's southern end.

In September 1892 a public fountain was erected on the Green, presented to the town by James Steven of Skeldon House, near Dalrymple. Steven had made his money in iron foundries, and the fountain was, naturally, made from cast iron. It is adorned with dolphins and an otter with a fish. After falling into disrepair, the fountain was refurbished by Kyle and Carrick District Council and rededicated on 6 June 1987.

A bandstand was erected in the middle of the northern end of the Green in the late Victorian period. Funds for this were raised over a time, including a charity football match held in 1887. An octagonal structure, it comprised iron pillars supporting a concave roof with cupola. The bandstand proved to be popular with residents and visitors alike. A burgh band was formed in 1907 and soon it was under the control of the Council. To entertain the visitors it performed at the bandstand as well as in Alloway's Tea Gardens during the summer months. The bandstand remained on the Green until the winter of 1951-2 when it was taken down and replaced by a shelter.

In 1893 the Council proposed erecting three stances on the

The original Victorian bandstand on the Low Green

Green, but the owner of Glendoon House (now Fairfield House) objected, as they would obscure his view of the sea. A wooden hut, leased to Petro Brucciano for the sale of ice cream, was also a problem. During the court case which followed, it was determined that under the terms of the title to the lands, the Council could not 'feu the ground', and thus the proposal to erect the stances came to nought. The Court of Session described the ice cream hut as 'a grievance and an eyesore'.

The Low Green remained about thirty-one acres in extent until 1910, but over the years a few corners were 'nibbled' away for development. A new putting green proved to be a popular attraction. In 1911 the Pavilion Theatre was erected next to Wellington Square, a massive Italianate building distinguished by its four square towers. In 1913 the theatre was leased to the Popplewell family who put on summer variety shows.

The threat of war in Europe led to the Council granting permission for the Royal Flying Corps to use the Low Green as a landing strip for their aeroplanes. The citizens of Ayr were not too pleased by this development, but accepted the situation until 1916 when the Corps moved their operations to the racecourse.

The Low Green has been used for demonstrations, meetings and other public events over the years. It was the scene of the start of a parade on 4 August 1919 to celebrate National Peace Day. After the Great War a tank, presented to Ayr Burgh Savings Committee, was positioned on the Low Green as a reminder of the conflict and to mark Britain's victory in Europe. The tank remained there until the Second World War when it was removed during National Savings Week in June 1940 and used for scrap iron in the war effort.

Improvements for the benefit of visitors were made in 1937-8. A new miniature car track, nicknamed 'Brooklands', was opened at the northern end of the Green. The old bandstand was replaced with a new facility. This comprised a stage measuring thirty by twenty-one feet that was capable of holding forty performers. The back of the stage faced the sea, and to the landward side was a hollowed amphitheatre within an enclosure that could accommodate an audience of fifteen hundred; the shell-shaped design was intended to produce good acoustics. Attached to the stand was a band room and storage space for chairs. The whole structure cost in the region of £2,900 to build.

Towards the end of the Second World War, Butlins, the well-known holiday company, had plans to acquire the Low Green and establish an amusement park there. Butlins intended to spend £15,000 on creating a park of four acres with associated buildings. They proposed a twenty-one-year lease, after which the park would become the property of the burgh. After much deliberation, and following a vote of twelve to six, the Town Council rejected these proposals. Butlins instead acquired the disused HMS Scotia camp near the Heads of Ayr, and converted it into a holiday camp.

In the early 1960s new developments came to the Low Green with the creation of a children's playground. Kiosks for the sale of ice cream and other seaside confectionery were erected, much to the delight of the many children who visited the Green. Parents welcomed the construction of shelters where they could sit while their children ran about in the sea breezes. With the assistance of the European Union, a more modern children's adventure area was created in 1995, enabling energetic youngsters to continue to enjoy the Low Green into the next century. This has an exciting climbing-frame with chutes and bridges, sandpit with various attractions, as well as picnic tables and seats to allow parents to watch their children. There may be more developments in the pipeline: South Ayrshire Council has ambitious plans to develop the seafront and surrounding areas, and the Low Green may be about to enter yet another new phase in its long history. Investment such as this will be welcomed by many residents, as well as the thousands of visitors to Ayr every year, who have great affection for the Low Green. We can only hope that this beautiful open space, enjoyed by local people for centuries, remains unsullied by development.

3
MANY A DEADLY FEUD

THE KENNEDY FAMILY OF Carrick was involved in many feuds in the sixteenth century and one of these spilled over from Carrick to Ayr, where murder was committed on the beach. The background to this incident could itself fill a book. The notorious murder amid the dunes happened when Sir Thomas Kennedy of Culzean left Greenan Castle for Ayr one morning in 1602. As he crossed the bay he was set upon by Sir Thomas Kennedy of Drummurchie and butchered to death.

Greenan Castle is perched precariously on a rocky headland to the south of Ayr. The origins of the castle are lost in time, but it has been claimed in recent years that it occupies an ancient fortified site that may have formed one of King Arthur's Camelots. The structure which walkers on Greenan shore see today probably dates from the late sixteenth century, built by the all-powerful Kennedy family, the so-called 'kings of Carrick'.

Sir Thomas Kennedy of Culzean was the second son of the 3rd Earl of Cassillis. He had fought at the Battle of Langside for Mary Queen of Scots, and was knighted at the coronation of Queen Anne in 1590. He was an extremely violent man, having acquired his wife by force in 1579. She was Elizabeth MacGill, daughter of the king's advocate, David MacGill, and ex-wife of Robert Logan, who was to be implicated in the Gowrie Conspiracy in 1600. Culzean and some armed followers came to the MacGill house when the father was absent and took Elizabeth by force. One month later they were called before the court, but Elizabeth stated that she went with Culzean by her own free will, and Thomas claimed that they had already married.

At the time of the murder the Kennedy family was embroiled

in a dispute, with the Bargany and Cassillis branches arguing over the chiefship, each family accusing the other of many crimes. The feud had its origin in 1570 when the 4th Earl of Cassillis is said to have roasted Alan Stewart, the Commendator of Crossraguel Abbey, in the black vault of Dunure Castle. The tale is suspect to some extent, but it is known that the Commendator was held against his will in Dunure Castle for nearly three months, during which time the Earl used cruel and violent measures to force a signature from him. Although Stewart was forced into signing over numerous lands to the Earl, the documents show that he did not lose out altogether. However, when Thomas Kennedy of Bargany arrived at Dunure with an armed force and freed the Commendator, he immediately revoked all the documents. The 4th Earl actually acquired most of the Crossraguel lands by purchase from James Stewart of Cardonald, to whom the Commendator had passed them. Shortly after this, in 1576, allegedly after falling from his horse (in rather suspicious circumstances), the Earl died.

The 5th Earl of Cassillis was only eight years of age when he succeeded. His father had made arrangements for the lad's maternal uncle, John, Lord Glamis, to be his tutor, much to the disgust of Sir Thomas Kennedy of Culzean. Sir Thomas had hoped to gain the position, but the 4th Earl could not trust him, for should the young lad die, Sir Thomas would inherit the estates and titles. Indeed, it was claimed that Sir Thomas and his men, disguised as Crawfurds of Kerse (long-standing enemies of the Kennedy family), rode into Maybole during the night and fired shots into the windows of Maybole Castle when Lady Cassillis was heavy with child, hoping to cause a miscarriage. Lord Glamis was killed in a brawl in Stirling in March 1579, whereupon Sir Thomas was appointed tutor, but just for one year, until the young Earl attained his majority.

In 1597 John Mure of Auchendrane (brother-in-law and supporter of Gilbert, 4th Earl of Cassillis) made what was supposed to have been a truce with Sir Thomas, but all the while he was still harbouring a grudge against the Cassillis side. Further attempts at reconciliation were made in 1600 when Helen, daughter of Sir Thomas, was married to James Mure, son of Auchendrane.

In the winter of 1601 Gilbert Kennedy of Bargany attempted to kill the 5th Earl of Cassillis by ambushing him, but the Earl managed to escape. A few days later, Cassillis had his revenge. Having heard that Bargany proposed travelling from Ayr to his home in the vale of Girvan on 11 December, he gathered a group of two hundred armed men together. Cassillis and his men left Maybole Castle and stood waiting at a spot known as the Lady Corse (Ladycross on modern maps), one mile north-west of Maybole. Bargany, who had but a small retinue with him, journeyed by a different route, and was able to spot Cassillis' men in the distance. Cassillis' force moved their position, following the opposite bank of the burn until a point was reached from where his men would have a clear view. Bargany crossed the burn, intending to fight, but discovered that only four men followed him – Mure of Auchendrane, Walter Mure of Cloncaird, James Bannatyne and Edward Irving. He is said to have remarked, 'Gude sirs, we are ower few!' The spot where the fight took place lies on West Enoch farm, where a mound once marked the site. In the struggle Bargany's followers were defeated.

An early account of the battle can be found in *The Historie of the Kennedyis*:

> Bot now, to speak of the nobill youthe, how gallantly he behaif-fit him selff, my penne can nocht writt the same; for being bot this way accompanyitt with their fywe menne, thair was against him the number of 30 horsemenne, quha all geiff the charge and straikis [strikes] to thir fywe. Yet quhan that thair wes of thame twa unhorssitt and ane slayne, sa that their wes nane with him but ane, yitt he wald nocht stay his curradge, bot raid through me Lordis menne, hard to me Lord, and cryit, 'quhair is me Lord him selff! Let him now keep promise and brek ane trie [break a tree]!'

The challenge was not taken up. Instead the forces struck at Bargany from behind, seriously wounding him. He was later taken to Maybole, still alive, and transferred to Ayr, where he died twenty-three hours after the fight. The historian gives a flattering description of Bargany:

He was the brawest manne that was to be gotten in ony land; of hiche stataur, and weill maid; his hair blak, bott of ane cumlie feace; the brawest horsemanne, and the best at all pastymis. For he was feerse and feirry, and wonder nembill. He was about the age of 25 yieris quhane he was slayne, bot of his aige the maist wyise he mycht be; for gif he had tyme to had experianse to his witt, he had been by his marrawis [marrows, i.e. companions].

In 1602 Sir Thomas Kennedy of Culzean sent a message to John Mure in which he proposed to meet him on the Ayr shore at a point known as the Duppill. *Dubh poll* translates from the Gaelic into Blackburn, a name more recognisable today. He set out from Culzean and rested at Greenan on the way. On 12 May Sir Thomas was met at the chosen location by Thomas Kennedy of Drummurchie, brother of Bargany, and five or six servants. They immediately killed him among the sand dunes. Culzean's body was robbed of a purse containing one thousand merks, his gold buttons and some items of jewellery. It has been claimed that John Mure of Auchendrane had put up Drummurchie to the murder, but nothing that could incriminate Mure was found.

The murder brought the 5th Earl of Cassillis and his brother, Hew, Master of Cassillis, closer together for a time. The Earl proposed that Hew should murder Mure of Auchendrane, for which he would reward him with 'tuelff hundreth merkis zeirlie [yearly]', according to a bond drawn up on 3 September 1602.

Lord Cassillis went to London in 1603 to take part in the coronation of James VI as James I of England. During his absence, on 21 May, his wife, Lady Jean, along with Hew, the Master of Cassillis, and their servants were attacked by a group of 'hagbutters' (soldiers with guns) and horsemen under Drummurchie and Mure of Auchendrane. They had been returning to Maybole from Galloway, but were forced to ride at speed to Auchinsoul House, near Barr, where they took refuge. Drummurchie immediately set fire to the building, refusing to release the occupants unless they first gave up one of their number who was accused of killing Gilbert Kennedy of Bargany. The Countess and the Master were eventually released on signing bonds guaranteeing large sums of money in payment to Mure and Kennedy, bonds which the Privy

Council later declared invalid. The man accused of the murder managed to escape the flames at Auchinsoul and fled to London, where he told Lord Cassillis of what had happened. The Earl flared up into 'ane readge'.

The messenger who had been sent by Kennedy to Mure, a young lad named William Dalrymple, was thought to know too much regarding the murder. Mure held him at Auchendrane for a while, but felt that he might manage to escape or even be found by raiders, so he was sent off to the Island of Arran for a time, and even served in Buccleuch's regiment in the Low Countries for five or six years. During Dalrymple's absence, Mure thought it safe enough to go to Edinburgh and present himself before the bar for trial. He also stated that he was willing to face any of Cassillis' men in combat who might challenge his innocence. The barefaced cheek of Mure was such that he was sent packing from the court with no trial.

When Dalrymple returned to Scotland, Auchendrane felt that there was still too much of a chance that he might speak, and so he arranged to have him murdered. His vassal, James Bannatyne, invited Dalrymple to his home at Chapeldonan, a few miles north of Girvan, where at midnight Mure the elder and Mure the younger entered and killed him. The corpse was taken down to the beach and buried in the sand. However, the tide was such that the sands were washed away, revealing the body. The Mures then arranged for a boat to take the corpse out into the bay, where it was thrown overboard. Despite the offshore winds, which were expected to take the corpse far from the place of the murder, the body appeared back on the beach.

A cry went out when the locals discovered the murdered corpse on the shore, and suspicions were quickly directed at Auchendrane. The Mures now regarded Bannatyne as knowing too much and the son decided that the best thing to do was to murder him also. Bannatyne became aware of the threat and, when the attempt was made to silence him forever, he managed to escape.

The evidence pointed to the two Mures of Auchendrane, who were arrested and locked up in Edinburgh tolbooth. Torture seems to have been used to try and force a confession from young Auchendrane, but 'he endured the torture with the utmost firmness, and by the constant audacity with which, in spite of his intolerable pain, he continued to assert his innocence, he spread so favourable an opinion of his case, that the detaining him in prison, instead of bringing him to open trial, was censured as severe and oppressive.' King James was so convinced of his guilt that he personally instructed the authorities to keep him in gaol even longer.

By this time Bannatyne had suffered severe pangs of conscience. He gave himself up to the Earl of Abercorn and confessed to his part in the murder of Dalrymple. At a trial in 1611 the two Mures and Bannatyne were found guilty, after evidence to support Bannatyne's tale (which the Mures denied strongly) was forthcoming. Mure the elder was convicted of counselling and directing Sir Thomas Kennedy's murder, as well as of the actual murder of Dalrymple. Bannatyne and Mure the younger were found guilty of their part in the murder of Dalrymple. All three were sentenced to be beheaded, but Bannatyne was awarded the King's pardon for coming forward and confessing.

Sir Walter Scott, in *Auchendrane, or the Ayrshire Tragedy*, used the story of the Carrick feud. In it he notes, ''Tis an old belief in Carrick here, where natives do not always die in bed, that if a Kennedy shall not attain Methuselah's last span, a Mure has slain him: such is the general creed of all their clan.'

4
THOU SHALT NOT SUFFER
A WITCH TO LIVE

SCOTLAND IN THE SIXTEENTH century was a place that feared evil in all its guises. The people of the countryside were highly superstitious and anything that could not be explained by normal Christian means was taken to be a sign of the Devil's work. St Paul's Epistle to the Hebrews in the New Testament enjoins, 'Thou shalt not suffer a witch to live,' and the Scots people followed the text to the letter. In 1563 the Scottish Parliament issued a law which stated that 'all who used witchcraft, sorcery, necromancy, or pretended skills therein, and all consulters of witches and sorcerers should be punished capitally.' Even King James VI was afraid of witches and in 1597 he wrote a book entitled *Daemonologie*, to help his subjects to identify witches and wizards and have them brought to trial.

In 1586 the witch of Barnweill was burned in Ayr. She had been accused of numerous misdemeanours in the parish of Craigie, before being caught and taken to the county town for trial. Naturally, she was found guilty and sentenced to die. The expenses for this execution were recorded in the burgh accounts: £7 3s 8d Scots for 'expenssis sustenit in the burning of the witche of Barnweill, in candillis, hir meit and drink, pyk barrellis, colis, rosat, heddir, treis and uthiris necessaris'.

In 1595 Marion Grief was burned as a witch in Ayr, her execution requiring coals, cords, tar barrels 'and other graith [equipment]' which cost £4 4s in total. In the same year Agnes Hucheon was charged with witchcraft but managed to escape execution, for she was found guilty of simply 'abusing' people. Nevertheless, she was punished by being whipped up and down the High Street, forced to wear the branks on two market days, along with a variety of other punishments, before the Presbytery was satisfied that she had repented. The branks was an iron ring that circled the head and had a spike which stuck into the open mouth, thus preventing the unfortunate wearer from speaking.

Susanna Shang was reported to the Kirk Session of Ayr as having possible witchcraft connections. The ministers were convinced of her guilt, and she was passed on to the Council who reported her name to the Lords of Council in Edinburgh. Application for a grant to try her was made, and no doubt received. In 1596 a Galloway woman, Margaret Reid, was suspected of witchcraft and was locked up in the tolbooth for six weeks. She was fed only bread and water and eventually released on a penalty of being banished from the county. The court declared that if she was 'ever found within their jurisdiction', she was 'to be punished without any further assize or process'.

Janet Young was burned to death in 1599. Her execution cost the burgh £5 7s 8d, of which 7s 8d was for a rope with which to tie her up, £1 for a barrel of tar, and £4 paid to Barquhill, the hangman, for carrying out the deed. Barquhill also executed Bessie Bell in 1613 at a cost of £4 11s 4d. In 1618 James Gilmour was the burgh lockman, or hangman, and he was paid £6 13s 4d for executing Maly Wilson. Janet MacAllister was executed in Ayr for witchcraft in the same year.

Janet Smyllie was a notorious witch from the first half of the seventeenth century. In 1613 she was noted for her slanderous speeches in which she decried many of the burgh's residents. When the authorities caught her she was tortured with the branks. She was then taken to the Fish Cross and locked up in the jougs where the passing public could make her suffer by throwing rotten food at her. On another occasion, in 1621, she is recorded as doing penance in the parish church. It is reported that she contemplated suicide after this, seen by the authorities as further proof of her guilt. Janet Smyllie was apprehended once more in 1628 and locked up in the women's cell that was located beneath the stairs of the tolbooth, where she was fed on bread and water. The following year a court was ordained and she was tried on a charge of witchcraft. Found guilty, she was sentenced to banishment outwith the county. However, Janet Smyllie returned to Ayr, for she is noted again in 1649. In that year she was locked up in the tolbooth and died. The Council asked the minister, William Adair, what they should do with her body. He advised them to tie it to a sledge and drag it along the street to the foot of the burgh gallows and there burn it to ashes.

It was reckoned that there were certain parts of a witch's body which felt no pain, and many 'witch-finders' established themselves all over the country to test this rather dubious theory. Suspect witches were tied and bound, and the witch-finders stabbed at their body with a large pin, trying to find some piece of skin where they seemed to experience no pain. In 1644 the Presbytery of Ayr considered employing a professional witch-finder from Galloway.

In 1650 Hugh Eccles, Moderator of Ayr Presbytery, applied to the Estates for a general commission against all witches, which would allow them to pursue and execute any suspected witches without further recourse to Edinburgh. By 11 June that year the Kirk Session had witches under lock and key, and a guard was placed on them to prevent them from falling asleep, as it was thought this would help in bringing about a confession. One of these possible witches was Bessie MacCallan, who had been suspected of witchcraft and locked up that year. What became of her is not known, but no doubt she was burned to death with the Presbytery's new-found powers.

Janet Saers (or Sawyers) was strangled at the stake in 1658 after which her corpse was burned to ashes. As she was dragged to her execution she protested loudly that she was innocent. One of the English soldiers stationed at the Citadel witnessed the event, and wrote sympathetically about the woman's plight.

The most famous witch connected with Ayr was Maggie Osborne. To the researcher she is quite an elusive character, as there was more than one woman bearing that name in the town. Some say that she was a daughter of the Laird of Fail, which would make her maiden name Wallace. According to tradition she lived at 78 High Street, opposite the Fish Cross, where she ran a tavern, the site of which was latterly occupied by the Osborne Bar. Records exist which note the Osborne family at that address, occupying what has been described as the 'Osborne mansion'. It stood three storeys in height on the south side of the Gadgirth Vennel, an old alleyway that led from the High Street to a ford across the river. According to William Robertson's *Historical Tales and Legends of Ayrshire*, 'The inhabitants could point out to strangers the house in which she resided, but Time's effacing fingers have swept it away and nothing more than the site is left.' It was demolished in 1881 and the Osborne Hotel erected in its place; Marks & Spencer currently occupies the site. The burgh records note payments being made to a Margaret Wallace or Osborne for wine between the years 1613 and 1623.

Many tales of Maggie's exploits were recounted in the burgh over the centuries, but have been lost in the mists of time. She had connections with Carrick and Galloway, for tradition claims that she would head off in those directions in the hours of darkness. An old pathway across Carrick Hill was known as 'Maggie's gate to Galloway'. Near the Rowantree Toll on the hill road between Newton Stewart and Straiton, is a spot known as Maggie Osborne's Bridge. In the nearby pass known as the Nick of the Balloch is another crossing known as the Witches Bridge. It was while in the vicinity that she noticed an approaching funeral party. Maggie knew the mourners, and did not wish to be recognised so far from home. Using her black arts she turned into a beetle, and lay on the road. Unfortunately a horse nearly stood on her, for which insult she decided to seek revenge. She caused an exceptional snowfall to land on a thatched roof, which collapsed on the residents within, killing most of the family. Another son was drowned when Maggie sank his ship in Ayr Bay.

A number of folk accused Maggie of evil deeds and eventually she was called before the courts. She was diagnosed as suffering from brain fever and being possessed by the Devil. Accordingly, Maggie was burned to death at the Malt Cross of Ayr, at the junction of the High Street with New Bridge Street. The 1856 Ordnance Survey map of the town even records that she 'was burned for Witchcraft at the end of the 16th Century'. The date of this may not be correct, for the Ayr Kirk Session records of 12 October 1629 make reference to the burning of Margaret Wallace. Others claim that she was burned sometime between 1652 and 1681, when the Session records are blank. The latter is possible, for there is a reference in the burgh records to a Maggie Osborne who was appointed 'to receave the key of the house wherein Isabell Pyper died under suspicione of the infectioune, fra John Fergusson, one of the quarter-masteris, and to intromit with the goods of the house and to be furthcumand to their said honours conforme to ane indenture thairof, to be taken and sett doun in wrytt'.

Tradition has it that Maggie's corpse was later taken to the kirkyard of St John's Tower and buried there. A stone long marked the grave, in recent years replaced by a wooden memorial, but both have now gone. Exactly why Maggie merited burial in a Christian site is another of her mysteries.

There were also men who were tried for crimes such as sorcery or fortune telling, but they were in general not persecuted with the ferocity that was dealt out to women accused of witchcraft. In 1582 William Gilmour of Polquhairn was called before the Lords of Council in Edinburgh on a charge of witchcraft and sorcery. He was sent to appear before the justiciar of Ayr but no further reference to him is known. In 1651 John Muir was banished for reading palms and making other predictions. A spaeman named Michael was excommunicated in 1623. As late as 1684, a dumb man was hauled before the burgh magistrates for pretending to tell fortunes and for predicting where items that had been lost could be found.

5
CROMWELL'S OCCUPATION

IN JANUARY 1652 the Cromwellian Administration took over the management of Scottish parliamentary affairs when Charles II fled into exile following his defeat at the Battle of Worcester. For the next six years Oliver Cromwell ruled Scotland as part of the republic, but when he died in 1658 and was succeeded by his son, Richard, as Lord Protector, the tight grip over the country was lost and the crown was restored to Charles II in 1660. During Cromwell's period in control a number of major changes were introduced in Scottish affairs, and Ayr was one of five towns selected as the location for a new fort. The others were built at Inverlochy (near Fort William), Inverness, Leith and Perth. These forts were established to subdue the country and to ensure their support for the commonwealth.

In Ayr a site between the town and the sea was considered ideal for the fort and work began in April 1652. Unfortunately this was also the location of the parish church of St John the Baptist, which had stood there for many centuries. This presented no real problem to Cromwell, as he simply requisitioned the church for his own use. The tall tower was ideal for a lookout, as it afforded fine views of the firth, the town inland and the harbour to the north. It was also used as an armoury and guard room. To compensate the inhabitants for the loss of their church, he granted one thousand English merks towards the cost of a new place of worship. A Deed of Gift was drawn up, the original document now hanging in the Auld Kirk of St John the Baptist. A modernised version reads:

> I do hereby testify that Major-General Deane did promise unto the Burgh of Ayr the sum of one thousand merks Sterling money

towards the building of a church in that town, by reason that their former church was employed for the public, and did give me order to pay £200 upon laying the foundation one foot above the ground, and £200 when it was half-build, and the remainder when it was finished. In testimony whereof I have hereunto set my hand this first day of August 1654.

The deed was signed by Colonel Matthew Alured and countersigned by Colonel Robert Overton. The latter added, 'I have perused the promise and do know and accept of the same to be true.'

It was at this time that the present Auld Kirk of St John was constructed, built by fine local stonemasons, John Masoun, who was later to be interred in the kirkyard which surrounds it, and John Smith, both from Kilmaurs. The contract for the construction is dated 16 June 1653, and the Reverend William Adair celebrated the first communion in the church on 22 September 1656. The site chosen for the church had previously been occupied by the Greyfriars' Monastery.

Hans Ewald Tessin, Cromwell's engineer, supplied a plan for the new fort. It comprised an elongated hexagon with six bastions at the corners. The walls facing the river were larger than the rest, the ground dropping steeply at this side. The walls are revetted, that is built on an angle and supported behind either by earth banks or arched masonry. In the latter case the vaults created were used for storage. The west side of the fort, which overlooks the sea, was formerly directly on the shore, but the sea has been pushed back somewhat from the time when the waves lapped at the base of the walls.

Long-standing tradition claims that the stones used in the construction of the fort were salvaged from Ardrossan Castle. It is said that the squared masonry was dragged from the Castle Hill to the coast and then ferried across Ayr Bay to Ayr harbour. Certainly the stone is similar to that used at Ardrossan, and to erect the fort walls in so short a period suggests that the stone was indeed second-hand. It is also the case that Ardrossan castle was a property of the Earl of Eglinton and, after the restoration of the crown, he asked for and was granted the right to the citadel of Ayr as compensation for his losses. It was at this time that the lands of the fort were created into a barony, named Montgomeriestoun after Eglinton's surname.

Construction of the fort was a very difficult process, and a letter of 11 August 1652 recorded some of the problems:

> Our fortification here goes on fast. After we get the foundation laid we are very much troubled with water, and have no earth but a shattering sand, that as we dig in one place another place falls upon us.

Outwith the walls, on the eastern and southern sides, a ditch was cut, which sometimes filled with water, but more often than not was dry, due to the permeability of the sandy loam. The outer side of the ditch had a second wall, known as the Moat Wall. Parts of this wall survived for many years marking the rear boundary of the New or Cathcart Church grounds.

A diagram of Cromwell's fort, built in the early 1650s

The main entrance to the fort was in the middle of the eastern wall, where an archway through the walls held a gate. This arch survives in Academy Lane, but over the years the level of the ground has risen considerably, so that today it is only four feet in height. Originally a mounted horseman could freely ride through it. The archway is decorated by a rather heavy moulding, and a square recess, which formerly existed above it, held the arms of the Commonwealth of Great Britain. A second means of entering or leaving the fort existed at the north-western corner. Known as the Sally Port, this was located in the re-entrant angle of the Milthouse bastion.

On entering the fort the soldiers found a large open space, extending to about twelve acres. On this was erected a number of buildings, in addition to the ancient church of St John. On passing through the sentry post, visitors were faced with the guardhouse. To its left were footmen's quarters. Most of St John's was used as a storehouse and malthouse. Part of the nave, however, was kept in use as a church meeting place. The south-eastern bastion had a smithy and tavern (or alehouse) within it. More barrack rooms for footmen and officers were arranged along the southern sides of the hexagon. Near the south-western bastion were a bakehouse, brewhouse and various stores. On the western side of the central market place or arena were the stables for horses, horsemen's quarters and privies. The main officers' quarters were at the northern side of the fort, along with the hospital. The north-eastern bastion, which occupied the site of Ayr Castle and was the highest point within the walls, was the site of a gun emplacement, a position from which the town and harbour could be guarded.

To supply the soldiers in residence at the fort with fresh water, two wells had been sunk within its walls. One of these was located at the southern end, next to a guard house and soldiers' quarters (approximately at the junction of Eglinton Terrace with Bruce Crescent). The other was to the north-west, adjoining the officers' quarters (at the north end of Eglinton Place).

The cost of constructing the fort was excessive, especially by seventeenth-century standards. It is said that when Cromwell was informed of the cost he is reputed to have replied, 'What, has it been made of silver?'

Colonel Matthew Alured was the first commander of the fort. He had five hundred men under his command but in the autumn of 1653 his regiment was posted elsewhere. A regiment under the command of Colonel Thomas Cooper then garrisoned the fort. Major-General Richard Deane, who was mentioned earlier, was killed in 1653 while fighting the Dutch.

Most of the foodstuff and provisions required to feed the soldiers and horses in the fort were brought in by ship. A record of 9 July 1652 notes that 'Divers barkes came into Air with provisions for the troops, four frigates and several vessels for their assistance.' The harbour, though busy in transporting goods for the soldiers, was not too busy with trade. In 1656, when a Commonwealth representative travelled around the country to standardise the weights and measures used by the customs men, he found only three ships, one of 100 tons displacement, the other two only of three and four tons.

Cromwell's soldiers were reputedly responsible for diverting the course of the River Doon. Originally the Doon did not enter the sea at what is now known as Doonfoot, but instead took a swing to the north, running behind high sand dunes for a distance of almost two miles before entering the sea somewhere near the Low Green. This explained why land of about fifty acres in extent at Cunning Park was included in the parish of Maybole. Whether the Doon was silting up the harbour or affecting the fort in some way is not known, but it is claimed that the soldiers dug a new channel for the river through the dunes, allowing it to reach the sea at its present embouchure. However, no confirmation of this theory has been found.

The soldiers were not always the well-drilled regiment they were expected to be. In 1656 two groups of soldiers were involved in a riot – one half was based in the citadel, the other was embarking at Ayr harbour for Jamaica. On other occasions the Kirk Session make reference to their misbehaviour. One of the soldiers had broken the burgh's social code and was publicly flogged through the streets.

In 1657 the wedding took place between one of Cromwell's soldiers and a local girl. Abe Shockley had been stationed at Ayr for some time and fell in love with one of the town's bonnie lasses, Margaret Campbell. Following a misdemeanour, Shockley had been reduced in rank and thrown out of the barracks. After he fell in love with Margaret he required permission to marry her, and also had to sign the Covenant to guarantee his orthodoxy.

A number of other men who arrived in Ayr with Cromwell's troops were to settle locally. John Hodgson was an English trader who settled here during that time. His assistant was another Englishman named Ralph Holland. He too married locally and established himself as a merchant. By coincidence, Holland's son,

William, and Hodgson's son-in-law, Captain Thomas Fullerton, were both drowned at sea whilst taking part in the Darien scheme.

With the restoration of the crown in 1660, Ayr citadel was abandoned. It lay unoccupied for three years until it was granted to the Earl of Eglinton as a Burgh of Regality. However, his plans for creating a town within it did not materialise. St John's, however, was used as a place of worship about thirty years later (1687-9), for King James's 'Indulgence' allowed the establishment of 'ye meeting house', where the Reverend William Eccles preached to supporters of the Covenant. The congregation later returned to the Auld Kirk. The citadel's moat was eventually filled in around 1800.

6

A SACRED NUMBER OF
TRIUMPHANT SAINTS

THE SEVENTEENTH CENTURY was a time of great turbulence and conflict in Scotland. King Charles I had tried to impose episcopacy on the country, to bring it into line with England, but the dour Scots Presbyterians would have none of it. The Cromwellian period offered a respite, but when Charles II was restored to the throne he started the process again. The National Covenant and the Solemn League and Covenant had been drawn up in support of presbyterianism against the King's wish to impose episcopacy on Scotland, but in 1662 Charles II declared the Covenants illegal, and demanded that all ministers inducted since 1649 should appear before his bishops and be re-ordained. Around one third of Scotland's ministers, about four hundred altogether, half of whom came from the south-west, refused to appear. As a result, they were ejected from their churches, and Episcopal ministers, or 'Curates' as they were known, were installed in their place. In Ayr these were George White, or Whyte, until 1682 and William Waltersone from 1682 until 1688.

Ayr was Covenanting in its sympathies, and there was considerable tension between the residents and the officials of the government. According to the Reverend William Wodrow, a toast to the Devil was drunk at the Malt Cross at midnight on Christmas Eve by some of the Earl of Middleton's soldiers (the Earl was Royal Commissioner to the Scottish Parliament and a supporter of episcopacy).

Many of the ousted ministers began to hold meetings in private houses. These were later declared to be illegal, and field-meetings, or Conventicles, were held instead. They are known to have taken place at the Cromwellian fort and at Gearholm, near Doonfoot. Soldiers were billeted throughout the country to search out those who attended these meetings, and if those caught failed to swear the Oath of Allegiance to the King then they could be hanged or shot on the spot.

The ministers of Ayr at the time, William Eccles and William Adair, both refused to accept that the Crown had authority over the Church. Adair was singled out by the authorities as one whom they wished to bend to their demands, in an attempt at frightening the rest into following suit. He capitulated and swore the oath as demanded. He refused to convert to episcopacy in 1670, however, and died in 1684.

In 1664 the councillors of Ayr were ordered to renounce the Covenants. The Provost, William Cunningham, acceded to this demand, as did nine of his councillors, but eight others refused and new councillors had to be found. Schoolmasters, too, had to conform to authority, and in 1675 William Wallace was dismissed. James Anderson followed in 1677 and William Rankin in 1680. To ensure that the populace attended the Curate's church, soldiers were quartered in the town to search out those notified to them by the Curates. A total of 450 men were billeted in the town, head-quartered at Newton Castle.

In November 1666 a group of Covenanters rose up against the authorities in the Stewartry of Kirkcudbright and began a march on Edinburgh where they intended putting their case before parliament. The route taken was a circuitous one, taking them from Carsphairn through Dalmellington to Ayr. Here Lieutenant Wallace of Auchans, a soldier of note, joined them and took command. By the time they reached Ayr their number had swollen to two thousand. The route to Edinburgh took them by way of Ochiltree, Muirkirk and Lanark. On the outskirts of the city the Covenanters had a change of heart, and skirted round the periphery of Edinburgh. Soldiers under the command of Sir Thomas Dalyell of the Binns eventually caught them up at Rullion Green, where a short battle resulted in about fifty deaths and thousands of arrests. Of those arrested, Ayr merchant Ralph Shiells was taken to Edinburgh where he was tried, found guilty and hanged.

The authorities decided that it would be of greater benefit if a number of the Covenanters were tried in the western counties, as a warning to anyone else who planned defying the law. Accordingly, a court was convened at Ayr, under the command of the Earl of Kellie, Lieutenant-General Sir William Drummond of Cromlix, James Crichton (brother of the Earl of Dumfries and Sheriff of Nithsdale) and Charles Maitland of Hatton (later Earl of Lauderdale). They met on 14 December 1666 and twelve Covenanters were placed in the dock.

The trial was a foregone conclusion: the Covenanters were all found guilty and sentenced to die. Two were to be hanged in Irvine, two in Dumfries, and the remaining eight in Ayr. It was at this point that the affair became a distinct problem for the authorities. The burgh hangman did not wish to carry out the executions, either because he was a supporter of the Covenant or because he could not bring himself to execute men who were willing to die for their religious beliefs. To avoid having to carry out the deed he absconded.

The authorities in Ayr sent to Irvine for a replacement hangman. He was one William Sutherland, a Highlander from Strathnaver, who had moved south in search of an education. He is first noted in Paisley where he earned a living by sweeping chimneys and hanging the odd witch or two. He then moved to Irvine where he volunteered to act as the burgh hangman, so long as the authorities there were willing to teach him how to read his Bible.

Irvine's Provost, Robert Cunningham, sent for Sutherland, but when he refused to carry out his wishes the Provost had him thrown in gaol. A guard then took him to Ayr, where again he was locked up in the tolbooth. George White, the burgh Curate, or Episcopal minister, spoke to Sutherland at length, giving him examples of Biblical precedents for killing others. Sutherland responded by quoting the Gospels. When his assiduous attempts at persuasion failed, White reluctantly gave up, declaring that Sutherland was possessed by the Devil.

The judges then tried persuasion of a different sort. Threats of torture were made. These included placing a cramp around his legs (the 'boot'), and threatening to pour boiling lead over his body. Lord Kellie ordered that he should be locked up in the stocks, where he was left for some time. Drummond then had him tied to a stake, and four soldiers were ordered to train their muskets on him. Sutherland was resolute, however, and would not give in. Eventually they, too, gave up and he was taken back to prison. After remaining locked up for a few weeks, he was released.

Sutherland afterwards wrote a 'Declaration', in which he detailed his tortures and trials. This, though 'rude, and in a very homely dress', was published on a number of occasions.

Then someone had the idea of asking the Covenanters if one of them was willing to execute the others, in return for being granted his freedom. The resolve of Cornelius Anderson, a tailor from Ayr, was wavering, and he asked the others if they would forgive him if he carried out the task. The others were willing to exonerate him, and so Anderson told the authorities that he would do their dirty work.

The burgh authorities had to ply Anderson with brandy before he could bring himself to carry out the executions. He hanged James Smith, Alexander MacMillan, James MacMillan, John Short, George MacCartney, John Graham and John Muirhead. These men came from all over the south-west of Scotland: James Smith was from the Old Clachan of Dalry in Galloway; Alexander MacMillan is sometimes referred to as Alexander MacCulloch – perhaps the mason made a mistake by giving us two MacMillans – and Alexander 'MacCulloch' is known to have come from Carsphairn; James MacMillan lived at a place named Marduchat, or Barduchat; John Short was another man from Dalry; George MacCartney farmed at Blairkennie; John Graham lived at Midtoun of Old Clachan of Dalry; and James Muirhead was a resident of Kirkpatrick Irongray.

The executions took place on 27 December 1666. The Covenanters were to be hanged, following which their heads and hands were to be removed and displayed in a public place as a reminder of what those who rebelled against authority should expect. The place of execution was probably at the Sandgate tolbooth, though this has been the subject of much debate over the years.

When Anderson had completed his work in Ayr the authorities took him to Irvine, where he hanged James Blackwood and John

MacCall on the same basis. They then let him go free. He was last heard of in Ireland, where he 'perished a wretched outcast'. Some say that he was burned to death in his own home, perhaps an act of suicide.

The bodies of the martyrs were taken to the old churchyard where a memorial stone, erected by the Incorporated Trades of Ayr, marks their grave. It reads:

> Here lie seven Martyrs for our Covenants,
> A sacred number of triumphant Saints,
> Pontius McAdam the unjust Sentence past,
> What is his own the world will know at last,
> And Herod Drummond caus'd their Heads affix,
> Heav'n keeps a record of the sixty-six.
> Boots, thumbkins, gibbets were in fashion then,
> LORD, let us never see such Days again.

The heads and hands remained on display for thirteen years thereafter, until they were taken down following the Covenanting victory at the Battle of Drumclog. At the same time the Council thought that things were beginning to swing to the side of the Covenanters, and had some prisoners released, but with the defeat at Bothwell Bridge a few weeks later they revoked their support. A few Ayr residents had taken part at Bothwell and, following their arrest, were sentenced to transportation to the Americas as slaves.

The Reverend Alexander Peden, ousted minister of New Luce in Wigtownshire, was held in Ayr tolbooth for a time in 1672-3. Money from the Kirk Session funds was used to feed him. Lord Rothes sent an arrest order to Major William Cockburn detailing what to do with him:

> Thes ar requyring you to order a pairtie of six hors and on to comand them to mairch to Aire and receive ye person of Mr Alexr Pedine, a rebell, in ye tolbuth there, and bring him in saiffe custodie to the tolbuthe of Edr. And this shal be warrant to ye keeper theroff to receive him and ye person of Hew Fargusone, allso prissoner ther and to you for ye bringing of them in, daited at the paleice off Halirudus, this 17th of Junij 1673: sic subscribitur,
>
> Rothes.

Peden was sent on to Edinburgh where he was sentenced to transportation to the colonies, but he was able to escape. He managed to avoid being captured again and died of natural causes on his brother's farm on Auchinleck estate. At first he was buried in Auchinleck churchyard but the soldiers, incensed at not having captured him, dug up his corpse and took it to Cumnock where they intended hanging it on the gallows tree. Fortunately, some prominent local citizens intervened to prevent this indignity, but his body was buried at the gallows foot 'out of contempt', according to the memorial which was later erected on the site.

In 1678 the Highland Host was sent to the south-west of Scotland. This was a group of poorly trained soldiers, recruited in the highland counties, who were billeted on folk under suspicion of being Covenanters. Ayr was selected as the headquarters for these highlanders, and Cunning Park House was taken over for this purpose. The hosts were expected to feed the highlanders billeted on them, and in many cases this left them penniless and destitute. The soldiers, too, abused their hosts on innumerable occasions, and when they were ordered to leave, they stole thousands of pounds worth of property. In fact, during their relatively short spell living in Ayr, it has been calculated they stole no less than £12,000 (Scots) worth of property.

In 1684 the heritors of the county were summoned to Ayr where they were to appear before a court held in the Auld Kirk. As they waited for their trial, the men were held either in the tolbooth, in the body of the kirk or else in the aisle. One by one they were asked to repeat the Test Oath, which acknowledged the King as having supremacy over the Church. Those who were willing to subscribe were let go; those who refused were held in prison for a time, before being released on payment of bail.

In 1684 another Covenanter suffered martyrdom at Ayr. He was Andrew MacGill, a native of Ballantrae. An informer by the name of Andrew Thom gave information to the soldiers about MacGill and his actions. He also told them where he could be found, and the dragoons were quick to arrest him. He was hauled back to Ayr where he was sentenced and hanged on the burgh gallows. MacGill merited no Christian burial in the eye of the authorities, and his corpse was buried at the gallows foot. For many years a memorial stone marked his grave, but this has long since disappeared, and numerous quests to discover what happened to it, or indeed where exactly it stood, have proved fruitless. The epitaph on the stone read:

Near this abhorred Tree a Sufferer lyes,
Who chus'd to fall, that falling Truth might rise,
His Station could advance no costly deed,
Save giving of a Life, the Lord did need.
When Christ shall vindicate his Way, he'll cast
The Doom that was pronounc'd in such a haste,
And Incorruption shall forget Disgrace
Design'd by the Interment in this Place.

After the government's victory over the Covenanters at Bothwell Bridge, John Graham of Claverhouse was presented with the Freedom of the Burgh of Ayr. This was not given lightly: indeed, it was said that the councillors were ordered to confer the dignity on him.

Robert Baillie of Jerviswood (near Lanark) was executed in Edinburgh in 1684 for his Covenanting adherence and his part in the Rye House Plot that had been conceived to assassinate Charles II. After the death sentence was carried out, his body was drawn and quartered, one of the quarters being sent for public display on Ayr tolbooth.

Charles II died in 1688 and James VII was expulsed in 1689. William and Mary were crowned as monarchs at the Glorious Revolution and religious freedom returned. In Ayr the Curates, Waltersone and Alexander Gregory, were 'rabbled', or thrown out of their charges. According to the Kirk Session minutes of 14 January 1689:

No session this day, nor sermon, nor collection last Sabbath, both the ministers being discharged to preach by ane armed partie of rebellious hillmen upon their perill.

William Eccles was reinstalled as the parish minister and, much to the relief of the citizens of Ayr, the 'killing times' came to an end.

7
KIRKYARD TALES

THE OLD CHURCHYARD WHICH surrounds the parish church of St John the Baptist is today a quiet place off the High Street, apparently forgotten in the hubbub of Ayr life. There, hemmed in between the shops and the river, stands the old church, surrounded by its graveyard, the tombstones of which tell the story of the town.

The church and its cemetery were founded in 1652-6, when Cromwell commandeered the older church of St John as part of his citadel. But the site chosen for the church was not unconnected with religion. Here, until the Reformation of 1558-9, stood the Greyfriars monastery. The Grey Friars, or Franciscans, arrived in Ayr by invitation in 1474, and in 1481 the Pope agreed to their building a friary. It has been speculated that an even older religious building occupied the site. Excavations in 1982 at the Buttermarket Close, which adjoins the kirkyard to the north, unearthed fragments of window tracery and coloured glass. The site of the Friars' Well is shown on old maps of the town. This was located in the kirkyard, near the wall separating it from the river, and tradition holds that the water within it was of the purest quality.

Dating from 1656 is the lychgate that guards the entrance to the churchyard from Kirk Port. Lychgates are more common in England and are comparatively rare in Scotland. It is entirely possible this one owes its origins to Cromwell's connection with the building of the church.

At the time of the church's foundation the plague was rife in the burgh. It came in various cycles, one of the more severe ones being in 1647. At that time the 'brethren of the kirk' (the elders) made a number of declarations, one of which was to encourage traders from outside the plague-stricken area to take goods into the affected area:

> The brethren, taking to there considera[tio]n the state and case of the towne of Air now afflicted by pestilence, were desyred to exhort there severall congrega[tio]ns, to furnish to the said towne, such comodities as they might spaire, vpon the charges of the said towne, vpon a moderat rate and the sellers of the said comodities within each Paroch to make choise of one day in the weeke for that effect and they to be accompanied with foure of the elders of there session, or other discreet men of the paroch, that so the present necessitie of the said towne may be suplied, and each broth[er] to remember the said towne in there prayers.

Early in the nineteenth century body snatching became a serious problem in the country. Around 1820 the demand for bodies for dissection in the universities considerably outstripped supply, and many professors were willing to pay for fresh corpses dug from the grave. Tales of newly buried bodies being stolen in the night and taken to Edinburgh or Glasgow abound, and such happenings were not unknown in Ayr.

In an effort to stop the robbing of graves, a number of initiatives were tried. One of the simplest was to watch the graveyard all night, and in a number of churchyards watch-houses were erected to give the guard a place to shelter. In Ayr the relatives of the deceased took it in turns to guard the grave for up to six weeks after the funeral, by which time the body was so decayed that it was of no use for dissection. At other times mort-safes were used to prevent coffins being unearthed after the funeral. These were heavy cast-iron frames that were clamped around the coffin and buried with it, making it too heavy to lift out again without considerable effort. Once the corpse had decayed sufficiently the grave was reopened and the mort-safe removed for use again. Mort-safes were in use at Ayr and Alloway, where examples of the device survive. The one used at Ayr hangs in the lychgate, which leads from the Kirk Port to the graveyard, and is dated 1816. Alloway's mort-safes lie within the ruins of the old church.

In 1829 an incident concerning body snatching caused a public outcry in Newton upon Ayr. We can do no better than quote the *Air Advertiser* of the time:

On the evening of Thursday last [10 December], three dead bodies, packed up in trunks, were, from the offensive smell emitted, found in a cart of one of the carriers to Glasgow residing in Newton-upon-Air; and, the circumstance having excited a considerable sensation, the Constables were ordered to take possession of them, and two persons by who it appeared the trunks were given to by the courier [sic], and who were on their way to Glasgow, were brought back. The matter was investigated and it was stated by the parties, brought back and examined, that the bodies were purchased in Ireland and conveyed in a vessel first to Stranraer, and then to Air, from whence again they were to be conveyed to Glasgow College. Information of the occurrence was transmitted to Edinburgh, but there being no reason to doubt the statement made by the persons claiming the bodies, orders were given to deliver them up. Whilst these steps were taken the dead bodies were locked up in the Town-house of Newton, and no violence occurred; but early on Tuesday morning, when the bodies were taken out and put in a chaise with the view of being carried to Glasgow, some individuals who, it seems, were on the watch, observed the circumstance and with the aid of others, in spite of the resistance of the persons to whom they were entrusted, the bodies were taken out and carried to the sea-side, and on the instant, buried within the sea-mark, and in the after part of the morning, they were raised again, and carried some miles off shore and sunk in the sea.

In June 1831 a number of graves were robbed at a graveyard in Newton upon Ayr. Again the *Air Advertiser* reported:

The resurrectionists have again been at work in the neighbourhood. From the appearance of the grave of a young person lately interred in the Newton burying ground, suspicion arose regarding the fate of the poor inhabitant below. To satisfy the relatives of the deceased, who were apprised of the circumstance, the grave was opened, and, on examining the coffin, it was discovered the body had been abstracted. This led to the belief that other graves might have been despoiled in a similar manner, and, accordingly, a number were opened, and not a few coffins found empty.

The body-snatching period came to an end in 1832 when the Anatomy (Scotland) Act was passed, allowing the supply of corpses to the universities to be improved, and the need for robbing graves ended.

As the body-snatching problem subsided a new worry arrived. In 1832 the Asiatic cholera spread throughout the country, killing many thousands of people. The first case noted in Ayr was on 19 July when a woman arrived from Glasgow with the disease, only to die within twenty-four hours. She had lodged in the Isle Lane (Hope Street), from where the disease spread like wildfire. Within one month eighty-two cases were reported, of which thirty-one were to end in death. In August the epidemic reached its peak, with the period 15-21 August having 229 cases and seventy-nine deaths. The high number of fatalities put pressure on the parish kirkyard, but unlike Kilmarnock, where a public park had to be used for a mass grave, the burial ground managed to cope. Nevertheless, the kirkyard was extended to the east of the church as a result of the number of burials. Ayr suffered a total of 205 deaths from cholera but, as it was regarded as a shameful disease of which to die, no memorial stone records this as the cause of death.

A wander round the old kirkyard reveals a number of interesting stones. Here are buried many notable citizens who made Ayr what it is today, and to lovers of the ancient burgh a visit is a must. On the west wall is a memorial to John Masoun, mason in Kilmaurs, who built the church in 1654.

It is not possible to mention here all those commemorated in the kirkyard. Here lies Brigadier-General James George Smith Neill (1810-1847). He was a hero of the relief of Lucknow, where he fell. There is a statue commemorating Neill in Wellington Square, where he was born. It was the work of Matthew Noble, and erected in 1859.

James Smith of Monkwood Grove lies in the kirkyard. His grave was 'erected by friends and admirers' and notes that he was the 'father of Scottish Botany'. Smith died on 1 January 1848 at the age of eighty-eight. The Reverend Dr William MacGill (1732-1807) was minister of the church and author of *Practical Essay on the Death of Christ*, which led to a serious charge of heresy placed against him.

The old kirkyard has many memorials that commemorate sailors and others associated with maritime activities. Here lies

Peter Smith, shipbuilder. His only son, William Cuthbert Smith was a marine architect who was lost at sea off the Cape of Good Hope on 29 December 1857 on a passage from Calcutta to London. He was only twenty-two years old. Captain Thomas Reid drowned at sea on 20 December 1820 aged thirty-seven. Undated is the memorial to 'Alexander MacAulay who was drowned at sea'. James Smellie was the first engineer on board the steamship *Ispahan* which was wrecked off Brest in France in 1872. Captain James MacNidder was lost with all his crew when the *Taymouth Castle* sank on its passage from Columbo to London in 1862. The memorial to George Salvador MacKenzie had at one time many visitors. He was a lieutenant and adjutant in the 22nd Regiment of the Bengal Native Infantry but was drowned off Barrackpore in 1844 at the age of twenty-five.

A number of Ayr's former provosts lie in the kirkyard. We will meet some of them in the chapter on Burns. Another is William Fullarton of Skeldon, advocate (1778-1838). He was a keen supporter of burgh reform, but not so well known as his nephew, Dr John Taylor (1805-1842), the noted Chartist and great Radical reformer, whose statue can be seen in Wallacetown cemetery where he is buried. According to Hugh Allan, writing on 'Ayr Half a Century Ago and Since' in the *Ayr Advertiser* in 1889, Fullarton 'left the management of the town's affairs very much in the hands of the Baillies'.

8
THERE WAS A LAD –
ROBERT BURNS

ROBERT BURNS WAS BORN on 25 January 1759 at Alloway, a village to the south of Ayr. The cottage where he spent his youth had been built by his father in 1756, when he feued seven acres of land from Dr Alexander Campbell of Ayr. It was originally named New Gardens Cottage, for William Burnes used it as the centre of a market garden. A few days after Robert's birth a severe gale blew down one gable of the building, requiring it to be rebuilt. The cottage still stands, revered the world over as Burns' Cottage. When only one day old, Burns was baptised at home by the Reverend William Dalrymple, minister of Ayr Auld Kirk.

William Burnes, the poet's father, was born at Clochnahill in Kincardineshire but had in 1748 moved to Edinburgh in search of work. Two years later he moved west to Ayrshire. At first he worked at Fairlie House, in the parish of Dundonald, but in 1752 he moved to Alloway, working at Doonside House for John Crawford. He later moved across the River Doon to work on the Doonholm estate as head gardener. Dr William Ferguson, who employed him, later became Provost of Ayr (1759-61 and 1763-5). In 1755-6 William Burnes was responsible for constructing a new road to link Alloway with what is now Doonfoot. Ayr Town Council paid him £50 for the work on this road, which is now known as Greenfield Avenue. At its western end is Greenan Bridge, now known as Doonfoot Bridge. The Earl of Cassillis, employing the masons Adam Smith and James Armour, erected the original bridge in 1772. Armour is thought to be the same person as Burns's father-in-law, and Burns would have been familiar with the name on the plaque long before he had any thought of marrying his daughter.

Robert began his formal schooling at the age of six. His father had travelled to Ayr where, in Simpson's Inn (the Black Bull Inn) in River Street, he interviewed the eighteen-year-old John Murdoch for the post of teacher at Alloway. He was required to produce a sample of his handwriting to prove that he was up to the job of teaching both Burns and some of his neighbours. Murdoch came highly recommended, being vouched for by David Tennant, a self-taught teacher from Alloway who was, at the time, English master at the Grammar School. Murdoch's school was located near Burns' Cottage, but was demolished in 1878. John Murdoch moved away from the district for a few years but returned in 1773 to take up a post as English master at Ayr Grammar School. Burns was sent there for three weeks in the autumn of 1765 to improve his English and French, and was taught a little Latin by William Robinson, writing master at the school. During the three weeks Burns attended the school he lodged with Murdoch at his home in the Sandgate. This house was demolished around 1894 and is now marked by a plaque on the wall of number 58. Murdoch left Ayr in 1776 and moved to London, where he died on 20 April 1824. He was buried in St Andrew's Gardens cemetery in Gray's Inn Road.

Burns's father was friendly with Alexander Paterson, rector of Ayr Grammar School. Like the poet's father, Paterson was a native of north-east Scotland. Paterson loaned books to William Burnes in order that young Robert could read and learn from them. Paterson died in 1768, but his widow continued to loan books to the Burns family.

In November 1765 William Burnes had become so successful as a market gardener that he was able to lease a smallholding from Dr Ferguson of Doonholm. The farm was Mount Oliphant, which extended to seventy acres lying to the east of Alloway. The lease began in Whitsun 1766 and Dr Ferguson loaned William Burnes £100 with which to buy stock. Burns's father did not give up Burns' Cottage when the family moved to Mount Oliphant. He rented it out to a variety of tenants until 4 August 1781 when the feu was transferred to the Incorporation of Shoemakers of Ayr. That organisation leased out the cottage as an alehouse, but its condition was beginning to deteriorate seriously.

Burns became friendly with many of Ayr's residents. He also mentioned many others in his poems. Major William Logan and his sister, Susan Logan, lived for many years at Park House, which stood to the east of Carrick Road, and after which Parkhouse Street is named. Both Logans were honoured by poems by Burns. William Logan received the *Epistle to Major Logan*, which ends:

> *Nae mair at present can I measure,*
> *An trowth! my rhymin ware's nae treasure;*
> *But when in Ayr, some half-hour's leisure,*
> > *Be't light, be't dark,*
> *Sir Bard will do himself the pleasure*
> > *To call at Park.*

Major Logan was a celebrated fiddle player, and is noted as a wit of some standing. Some of the humorous anecdotes attributed to him are also attributed to Hugh Logan of Logan in Old Cumnock, the surname obviously causing confusion.

Burns sent Miss Susan Logan, the Major's sister, a copy of *The Minstrel* by James Beattie as a new-year gift in 1787, along with some verses entitled *To Miss Logan*:

> *Again the silent wheels of time*
> > *Their annual round have driv'n,*
> *And you, tho scarce in maiden prime,*
> > *Are so much nearer Heav'n.*

One of the Bard's best-known poems is *The Brigs of Ayr*, in which the Auld Brig and the New Bridge argue over who is the best. The New Bridge which Burns refers to in the poem is not the present new bridge, but the earlier Adam-designed structure which was erected in 1786-8 and collapsed in a storm in 1877. Burns predicted this in the poem, for the Auld Brig states that it would still be standing when the New Bridge was but 'a shapeless cairn':

As yet ye little ken about the matter,
But twa-three winters will inform ye better.
When heavy, dark, continued, a'-day rains,
Wi' deepening deluges o'erflow the plains . . .

Then down ye'll hurl, (deil nor ye never rise!)
And dash the gumlie jaups up to the pouring skies!
A lesson sadly teaching, to your cost,
The Architecture's noble art is lost!

The poem makes mention of a number of Ayr landmarks, some of which are long gone, while others have survived. Simpson's Inn, where Burns's father interviewed Murdoch, is mentioned, and in a footnote to the poems Burns explained that it was 'a noted tavern at the Auld Brig end'. Burns was a regular customer, and in September 1786 wrote a letter from there to John Ballantine in Ayr, enclosing a copy of *The Brigs of Ayr*. Another place mentioned in the poem is the Wallace Tower, but this referred to the older tower, which was replaced by the present gothic structure in 1834.

One artist's interpretation of Burns's great poem, *To a Louse*

Tam o' Shanter is regarded as the finest of Burns's poems. It tells the tale of Tam who was immersed in the business of drinking at an Ayr inn on market day. When he eventually decides to ride home he is astonished by the spectacle of dancing witches at Alloway's Auld Kirk. Forcing his mare into a gallop, he manages to escape the clutches of the witches as he crosses the keystone of the Auld Brig o' Doon. Unfortunately the witches were able to grab a hold of the horse's tail, wrenching

46

most of the hair from it. A cobble on the floor of the bridge was reputedly marked by the hoof-print of the grey mare, Meg.

The Tam o' Shanter Inn is the oldest surviving building in the High Street, readily discernible by its thatched roof. The building dates from 1748 and certainly has been an inn for many years, but in all probability only acquired its name when an enterprising landlord decided to capitalise on the popularity of Burns. The inn was converted into a museum in 1957, but in 1994 was restored to function as a public house once more.

Tam's ride to Alloway mentions a few places that can still be found. At Cairn Crescent in Alloway stands a small stone cairn marking the spot 'where hunters fand the murder'd bairn'. There was a prehistoric cairn on this site, but it was removed when the area was developed for housing. Within it a Bronze Age burial kist was discovered. The present cairn was erected in July 1965 by the builders, John Dickie and Son, the Burns Federation and Ayr Town Council.

In the same area is the well where 'Mungo's mither hang'd hersel', which is commemorated in a house in Shanter Way known as Mungo's Well. The well itself still survives, though is difficult to find. In the nineteenth century the landlord of the Burns Arms Inn, latterly the Burns Monument Hotel and now the Brig o' Doon Hotel, collected water from here and took it to Ayr by horse and cart. The water was sold at various points in the town.

Alloway Kirk is celebrated as the spot where the witches danced in great delight. The church was a ruin in Burns's day, though an engraving of 1789 by Captain Frances Grose shows part of the roof timbers still surviving. In the graveyard is the resting place of Burns's parents, William Burnes and Agnes Brown. Souvenir hunters broke the original memorial, and took parts of it away. The second headstone was also destroyed, and the present memorial is the third. Here also lies Isabella Burns Begg, the poet's younger sister. She lived until her death in 1858 in Bridge House, which stood near the present entrance to Belleisle Park.

The Auld Kirk of Ayr was the church to which Burns and his parents walked each Sunday. Burns refers to the minister, the

Reverend Dr Dalrymple, in some of his poems, including *The Kirk's Alarm*, where he is styled 'Dalrymple mild'. He is buried in the churchyard, as is the Reverend Dr William MacGill, 'one of the worthiest, as well as one of the ablest, of the whole priesthood', according to Burns.

In the lychgate of the church is a board that details other acquaintances of the poet who are buried in the kirkyard. These include Robert Aiken, a lawyer in the town and his first patron. Another patron buried here was Provost John Ballantine of Castlehill. William Ferguson of Doonholm, who helped to set Burns's father up in farming, also lies in the kirkyard. Buried here too is Dr George Charles, who was once a young playmate of the poet and who also became provost for a time. Here also lies David MacWhinnie, the Ayr lawyer who bought twenty copies of the original Kilmarnock edition, some relatives of John Wilson, the original of Burns's 'Dr Hornbook', and John Kennedy, 'keeper of the drowsy Dungeon clock'.

There are a number of memorials to Robert Burns in and around Ayr and Alloway. The oldest, and most famous, is the memorial at Alloway, located in attractive gardens near the Auld Brig o' Doon. This monument comprises a classical temple, the base of which has three sides, over which rise nine Corinthian pillars supporting an entablature and cupola. The very top of the memorial has a tripod, supported by three inverted dolphins, rising to a maximum height of seventy feet. The triangular base was selected to represent the three ancient divisions of Ayrshire – Kyle, Carrick and Cunninghame. The nine pillars represent the nine muses. Thomas Hamilton Junior was the architect responsible for the memorial. He was later to design a very similar memorial to Burns in Edinburgh, erected in 1830. This similarity resulted in claims that he was defrauding the capital by giving them a second-hand design.

That the monument was erected owes much to one man, Sir Alexander Boswell of Auchinleck. He was the son of the famous James Boswell, diarist and author, celebrated for his *Life of Samuel Johnson*. James Boswell and Burns were contemporaries, but they never actually met. Sir Alexander was a poet and writer too, and republished a number of rare books at his press in Auchinleck.

Sir Alexander was keen to erect a memorial to Burns at his birthplace in Alloway. He advertised a public meeting which all interested parties were invited to attend, to be held in Ayr on 24 March 1814. Unfortunately, only two people turned up – Sir Alexander and the Reverend Hamilton Paul. Undaunted, Sir Alexander went ahead with his proposed speech. The meeting carried on as if the hall were packed, and at the end Paul, who had been appointed secretary of the memorial committee, offered Boswell a vote of thanks. The minutes of the 'public' meeting were written up and printed in the *Ayr Advertiser* on 31 March 1814. In the intervening week Boswell had been busily contacting a number of important county gentlemen who agreed to form a committee, so that their names were included. Slowly funds began to trickle in, and Hamilton was engaged to furnish a plan. Eventually seven hundred subscribers came forward (of whom only one was female – Lady Hamilton Cathcart) and £2,000 was raised. Among those donating funds was the Prince Regent, later George IV, who contributed fifty guineas. About one third of the total came from overseas. The foundation stone was laid with full Masonic honours by Sir Alexander on Burns's birthday, 25 January 1820. Representatives from many lodges were present in the large crowd. The monument was unveiled on 23 July 1823. Tragically, Sir Alexander was unable to be present, for James Stuart the Younger of Dunearn had killed him in a duel earlier that year.

A local sculptor, James Thom (1802-1850), carved figures depicting Tam o' Shanter and Souter Johnie, which were exhibited around Britain. The money raised was sufficient to allow some ground around the memorial to be acquired and laid out as a garden. A statue house was added in the grounds around 1832.

A statue of Burns was unveiled in the newly created Burns' Statue Square on 8 July 1891. It was the gift of Ayr Burns Club to the town, and when it was unveiled by Sir Archibald Campbell, Lord Blythswood, it was estimated that more than forty thousand people turned up to witness the ceremony. The square was formed when the new railway station was redeveloped and the road from the town to the east had to be re-routed. The statue was the work of George A. Lawson. It stands on a pedestal of Aberdeen granite designed by James A. Morris (1857-1942), one of Ayr's finest architects and author of *The Auld Toon o' Ayr*. On the statue are bronze panels depicting Burns parting from 'Highland Mary', as well as scenes from *Tam o' Shanter*, *The Cottar's Saturday Night* and *The Jolly Beggars*. Fine wrought-iron railings that were the gift of Sir William Arrol formerly surrounded the monument.

Memorials to Burns can also be seen inside Alloway village hall. Panels on the wall depict scenes from *The Deil's awa' wi' the Exciseman* and *The Jolly Beggars*. These were the work of Pilkington Jackson. A statuette of the bard is located in a niche in the wall.

When the Incorporation of Shoemakers bought Burns' Cottage, they converted it into an inn, and it existed as such for many years. Many notables have made a pilgrimage to the birthplace of the poet, including other famous writers such as Wordsworth and Keats. Both of them wrote poems about their visit, though neither is classed as a good example of their work. Early visitors to the birthplace were unimpressed. Keats described the landlord as 'a mahogany-faced old jackass who knew Burns – he ought to have been kicked for having spoken to him.' *The Glasgow Chronicle* of 1825 details what visitors could expect:

> [The Landlord] points out the bed in which the poet was born – shows a small bust he keeps in one room which was presented by Elias Cathcart, Esq., when he visited the cottage along with Mr Stewart of Dunearn, and several other gentlemen, and in another an admirable painting of Burns, which is 3 feet 8 inches on the canvas, by 3 feet across, and which was presented to the house above 20 years ago by Provost Ballantine. This completes Mr Gowdie's task. Not a single anecdote does he tell of Burns; he makes no pretensions to literature; and after an hour's conversation, a person leaves him, doubtful whether he ever read even a line of the poet's works.

The very first Burns Supper took place in the cottage in 1801. Nine men were present, all aficionados of the poet's work, and most of them known to him. They were Robert Aiken, lawyer, John Ballantine of Castlehill, William Crawford of Doonside, Dr Patrick Douglas of Garrallan, Hugh Ferguson of Ayr barracks, Thomas Jackson, rector of Ayr Academy, Primrose Kennedy of Drummellan, the Reverend Hamilton Paul and David Scott, banker. According to Hamilton Paul:

> The company of nine sat down to a comfortable dinner, of which sheep's head and haggis formed an interesting part. . . . Before breaking up, the company unanimously resolved that the Anniversary of Burns should be regularly celebrated, and that the meeing should take place on 29th January, the supposed birthday of the Poet.

The error in Burns's birth date was made in the first biography of the poet, and was not corrected for a few years. Those attending the supper presented a portrait of the bard to the Incorporation of Shoemakers for use as an external sign. Hamilton Paul, a noted musician and himself an author, composed a poem, *Ode on the Anniversary of Burns*.

At the second Burns' Supper, the nine men returned to the cottage, to be joined by nine others, including William Bowie, Provost of Ayr at that time. By 1810 the band of the Argyll Militia attended the cottage on his birthday, playing a number of airs.

In 1881 the cottage was acquired by the Burns Monument Trustees and restored to how it might have looked in Burns's day. A museum containing many important manuscripts and relics was built alongside the cottage in 1900. Here are preserved the family Bible, first editions of his poems, his journal of a highland tour, holograph letters and other artefacts. There are also portraits and busts on display, one of the busts being the work of Sir John Steell.

9
FREE TRADE IN THE BURGH

THE CONSEQUENCE OF VARIATIONS in taxation between Scotland, England and Ireland is that smuggling has frequently been a highly lucrative activity. At one time basic commodities such as salt were smuggled into the country, and in 1738 the owners of the salt works in Ayrshire complained to the Customs Board about illegal imports affecting their trade. We more often think of smuggled goods as being wine or spirits brought from abroad. However, contraband need not even come from foreign climes; home-produced whisky was often smuggled from the western isles into the heart of Scotland.

Ayr being a seaport has resulted in its being associated with the 'free trade', as smuggling was euphemistically called. Many accounts of smuggling in the town have been preserved, and many more survive in folklore. The town had its own custom house, a rather fine bow-fronted building in Fort Street erected in 1775. The customs collector at Ayr was responsible for the coast from near Troon south through the wild Carrick shore where many small vessels landed smuggled goods. One of the revenue boats based at Ayr was the *Vulcan*, which had thirty-one of a crew.

One of Ayr's oldest businesses has its origins in the smuggling trade. Alexander Oliphant and Company set up as an importer of wine in 1766. However, it has been discovered that the business was the legitimate front for a partnership that brought in more wine illegally than it did by fair means. The Company imported wines from Barcelona, Bordeaux, Cadiz, Guernsey, Lisbon, Madeira and Oporto and sent it on to branches in Glasgow, Kilmarnock, Moffat and Stranraer.

The Alexander Oliphant after whom the business is named

was formerly a landwaiter in the customs service. A landwaiter was employed to supervise the unloading of cargoes from foreign ports, and Oliphant was employed in the Ayr precinct from September 1742. Due to some incident or other, Oliphant was dismissed from the service in July 1760. His name added a sense of respectability to what was a business with many dark secrets. At its formation, Oliphant and Company had eight partners, a number of whom were known be connected with the smuggling trade. These included David MacClure of Shawwood, John Christian of Cunning Park and George MacCree of Picton. Other partners were Gilbert MacAdam of Merkland, John Campbell of Wellwood, Robert Whiteside, merchant in Ayr, and William Logan of Castlemains.

At the Portuguese town of Oporto in 1769 the customs men seized Oliphant's vessel, the *Buck*. The crew had smuggled tobacco on board but were caught red-handed. They were thrown in gaol and not freed until the following year. Whilst the men served their time abroad, their wives in Ayr often went to Oliphant's office to protest at the Company's lack of action.

David MacClure was the proprietor of a shipping firm based in Ayr. He was born in Dailly in 1733 and at the age of twenty-six was appointed a burgess of Ayr. He imported a variety of smuggled goods that came via the Isle of Man, where he had a number of business contacts. In March 1785 one of his sloops anchored off Port William in Wigtownshire and discharged a cargo of tobacco that the Wigtown collector reckoned was destined for Ayrshire. It was discovered that MacClure had been on board the vessel for a number of months as it sailed to Virginia and back via Ireland. MacClure was rich enough to become a shareholder in the Ayr Bank, although he lost £45,000 in that venture. He moved south to Liverpool where he set up a new business, and died in 1799.

John Christian came to Ayr from the Isle of Man in 1769 and set up home in the town. He was a known smuggler and like MacClure was able to purchase shares in the Ayr Bank. Not only that, he was appointed as the Bank's cashier. The Bank, after it had collapsed, was accused of having too many associations with the smuggling fraternity.

Whether Oliphant still had sufficient connection with the customs service in order to avoid detection is not known, but the Company had virtually no convictions for smuggling. The only one known was a minor incident when the firm imported French wine via Guernsey, but passed it off as Spanish wine (on which the duty was considerably lower) to the customs. This took place in 1767, and a letter survives with the instruction to 'clear it out and ship it under the denomination of Spanish Galicia. We must request you'll keep this to yourself. You need not even let the captain [John MacGowan of the *Hercules* of Ayr] into the secret.' Oliphant and Company was subsequently taken over and became Whigham's of Ayr, itself taken over by Corney and Barrow of London in recent years.

A number of Ayr vessels are recorded in the customs minutes books as having smuggled goods ashore. The *Jenny & Grizzy* of Ayr was captained by Malcolm Fisher. He is known to have landed in Ayr from France in 1764 with a cargo of brandy and wine, but informed the customs officer it was bound for Ireland. He also let it be known that he was heading for the Isle of Man on his way to Ireland, and had admitted that he landed at a Manx harbour en route to Ayr. The connection was enough to suggest to the excisemen that Fisher planned running the cargo ashore somewhere in Carrick. Further conversations with the crew, perhaps when they were in their cups, revealed that the captain had proposed landing the wine in some quiet creek, but that the revenue cutters, out in Ayr Bay, had prevented this from taking place.

In 1792 the sloop *Peggy & Nancy* of Ayr, captained by Robert Wilson, was seized in Kilbrannan Sound, the stretch of water between Arran and Kintyre, by the revenue officers. A scuffle ensued, in which the smugglers managed to retake the vessel. They put three of the officers on board the sloop's yawl, but in the rough and tumble of the movement it capsized and one of them, a Mr MacNeight, was drowned. The revenue cutter fired at the smugglers' vessel, causing it to drop its sails, after which it was accompanied to the harbour at Campbeltown. The ten smugglers were taken to gaol, and after questioning seven were released. Later, one of the smugglers, named King, managed to break out of gaol whilst the guards were drunk. A few weeks later Robert Wilson managed to escape and a few days after that Stewart 'cut the floor of the gaol from whence he lowered himself to the room underneath, where our courts are held, and having raised the window thereof effected his escape'. There is no evidence of the smugglers ever being recaptured.

It was not just goods landed at Ayr that the customs men had to deal with. In 1765 the smugglers were so brazen that they transported goods from Galloway to Glasgow through the town. The collector of customs at Ayr reported to the Board of Customs in Edinburgh:

> Notwithstanding the cruisers and other preventive vessels stationed on this and neighbouring coasts, it is very evident that wherries and boats with prohibited and high duty goods from the Isle of Man and other places do frequently escape them. For we have been lately told of great numbers of horses going through the country, even in the daytime, with two casks upon each and other packages, which had the appearance of teas, silk and other fine goods, and that the drivers of these horses, to the number of thirty or forty and sometimes one hundred, going together in one road, have all got firearms and other offensive weapons in order to beat off an inferior number of officers, when they find them unsupported by military force. And indeed were all the officers of the customs and excise in this district collected on such an occasion, we doubt if a less number of smugglers than mentioned could be overpowered and the goods secured, without the aid of the military. . . . [There was a recent case] of their having had the boldness of coming in daylight through the village of Girvan and thence passing the ford a little above the bridge of Ayr, a very public place, with about thirty horses all loaded with small casks and so proceeded to the Glasgow road, well knowing there were no soldiers here to be got by the officers [of the customs], either to stop or pursue them . . .

Smuggled goods were often landed at the Heads of Ayr. The Irish Revenue Commissioners were even aware of the 'Heads of Air' as an important location for landing cargoes. In November 1766 the revenue sloop *Prince of Wales* came alongside the *Mary & Ann* off the Heads of Ayr. On it was found a large quantity of arms and ammunition and the customs officers were convinced of the crew's part in running a cargo of illicit spirits on to the shore at Troon Point. By the 1770s the customs officers had made so many seizures in the Troon area that the smugglers moved southward towards the Heads of Ayr and Carrick. The customs officer noted that in December 1776 no fewer than four vessels were expected to land there.

Robert Burns had connections with the smugglers. As a lad he and his brother Gilbert played with the four sons of Andrew MacCulloch in Ayr, 'who kept a tea-shop, and had made a little money in the contraband trade, very common at that time', according to Gilbert Burns. Ironically, Robert Burns was later to become an exciseman himself, based in Galloway.

In the eighteenth and nineteenth centuries illicit whisky was smuggled from remote stills in the Highlands. Although distant in geographical terms from the Highlands, Ayr was one of the places connected with this trade, as boats could easily cross the firth from Argyll. When the illicit trade was at its peak, malt whisky from stills in Arran, Kintyre and beyond was smuggled into the town and sold on the black market.

On 18 January 1801 a group of excisemen left the port of Ayr for the island of Arran on board the revenue cutter *Prince Augustus Frederick*. The party included Captain Dowie, the ship's master, James Craig, supervisor of the excise at Ayr, two officers, Alexander Williamson and William MacLean, and a party of the 10th, or Edinburgh, Militia. On Arran they discovered seven illicit stills and five illicit maltsters, and seized three large stills. These were taken back to Ayr where they were locked up in the excise office. According to the report in the *Glasgow Courier* of 3 February 1801, 'Prosecutions against the offenders will immediately take place, who justly merit, in times of such dearth and scarcity, the most exemplary punishment the law can inflict.'

The historian James Paterson spent some of his youth in lodgings in Ayr. He often had to share his room with sailors from Arran. On many a night Paterson discovered that there were kegs below his bed, and on further investigation discovered that they contained 'Arran Water', as the illicit produce was euphemistically styled. It turned out that his landlady, who was renowned for her good quality whisky, had been supplying her regulars with illicit malt from Arran. Her customers were known to have included the Sheriff of Ayr! In 1851 a seizure of whisky was made, smuggled into Ayr harbour from Arran. After that it appears that smuggling on the Ayrshire coast died out. Or has it?

10

THE AYR BANK CRASH

ONE OF THE BIGGEST disasters to hit the town of Ayr, and the county which bears its name, was the Ayr Bank crash. This occurred in 1772 when the Ayr Bank of Douglas, Heron and Co. went bankrupt, leaving many of its shareholders in considerable financial hardship. Many notable Scots writers commented on the crash, including Burns, Boswell and Adam Smith.

Douglas, Heron and Co. was founded in 1769 by 136 partners. The Ayr headquarters was opened on 6 November that year and within a few days branches were opened in Dumfries and Edinburgh. The Bank had £150,000 worth of capital, but it also issued its own notes, to the value of £200,000. At one time it was reckoned that almost two-thirds of all the notes in circulation in Scotland were Ayr Bank notes. With the establishment of a branch in Edinburgh, the Bank had its sights set on being a national player. Its motto, *Pro Bono Publico*, means 'for the good of the people'. In addition to the branches established by the Bank, agencies were set up in many provincial towns, including Campbeltown, Glasgow, Inveraray, Inverness, Kelso and Montrose.

The Ayr Bank's backers were principally landowners. Indeed, it has been estimated that the value of land owned by its shareholders was worth between £3 and 4 million. Each partner could hold between one and four shares, worth £500 each. The principal shareholders were the Douglas family, in particular the Dukes of Queensberry and Buccleuch, the Earl of March, and Archibald Douglas of Douglas. Patrick Heron of Heron (c.1736-1803) was the second most important partner. He was later to become MP for the Stewartry of Kirkcudbright. Robert Burns wrote a number of satirical ballads to help his election campaigns:

The Douglas and the Heron's name,
We set at nought to their score;
The Douglas and the Heron's name,
Had felt our weight before.

It has been calculated that at least fifty-seven Ayrshire landowners held shares, including the Earl of Dumfries, John Campbell of Wellwood, Adam Fergusson of Kilkerran, Hugh Logan of that Ilk and Robert Ferguson of Castlehill. A number of Ayr businessmen and local dignitaries were shareholders. Among them were merchants like John Christian, David Ferguson, David MacClure, George MacCree and Robert Whiteside; the lawyers, John Boswell and John Murdoch; Dr Patrick Douglas of Garrallan, surgeon, George Dunlop of MacNairston, bank-teller, Claud Thomson, collector of the excise; and the Reverend William MacGill, minister of the New Church.

The loans offered by the Bank were intended for developing Scottish agriculture and industry, but instead many of them were used to fund the speculative purchase of plantations in the West Indies or for building town houses in Edinburgh.

In May 1770 the Ayr Bank was accused of 'note-picking' by the Aberdeen Banking Co. Note-picking was the practice of picking up notes from other banks and replacing them with your own. The notes from the other banks were then presented to them, and specie, or money in gold or coin form, was demanded from the rival bank's head office. This often cleared the bank out of hard cash, leaving it in a strained condition. The Ayr Bank was not alone in deploying this tactic; indeed, almost all of the provincial banking companies were accused of it.

In its first couple of years of business, the Ayr Bank was highly acquisitive in nature. In 1771 John MacAdam and Co. was taken over at a cost of £18,000. That bank had been founded by fifteen shareholders in 1763 with a capital of £15,000. Later in the same year the Dumfries Bank of Johnston, Lawson and Co. was acquired at a cost of £7,350.

The Bank's initial success was quite remarkable. It is claimed that it had forty per cent of all liabilities in Scotland at one time.

A number of major companies were debtors, notably the famous Carron Company of Stenhouse, near Falkirk. The Court of Session in Edinburgh was one of the Bank's most significant depositors.

£1 note issued by the ill-fated Ayr Bank of Douglas Heron and Co.

The drawing of bills on London banks to meet the cost of repaying notes grew to such an extent that it brought the downfall of the Bank. The London loans were costing the Bank eight per cent, whereas loans issued by the Bank to borrowers in Scotland were offered at five per cent. A London bank collapsed in early June 1772, sending shock waves throughout the country. Soon rumours spread that the Ayr Bank was likely to follow, and there was a sudden demand for cash in exchange for Ayr Bank notes. The Bank, in an attempt to prevent imminent collapse, placed advertisements in the newspapers offering £100 reward for information leading to the conviction of whoever was responsible for spreading rumours about the imminent demise.

The Bank was forced to stop payment on its notes on 25 June 1772. A notice was placed in the newspapers informing the public of the suspension of payment, but assured them that five per cent interest would still be forthcoming for those who held its notes. The Bank had plans to reopen in three months' time, but it never did. Most of its customers held on to their notes, knowing that a number of the Ayr Bank shareholders were wealthy enough to meet all the Bank's debts. At that time the Bank owed London businesses £600,000. It also owed £200,000 to cover the cost of its notes in circulation. A further £300,000 was owed to creditors who had loaned the Bank money.

In August 1773 it was decided to liquidate the Bank. However, this process went at such a slow pace that a Committee of Inquiry was appointed in July 1776. Its report was issued the following year, and recommended that the partners sue the directors for mismanagement. As a result nine actions were raised against sixty-one directors.

The principal cause of the failure of the Bank was its loans policy. These were mainly of a long-term nature, so that the notes issued on the back of the interest received were being returned for payment long before the loans provided a return. It was also true to say that many of the loans were offered to its own shareholders. These were often equal in value to the shareholding. The compilers of the *New Statistical Account* explained the problem:

> In consequence of the ultra-liberality of the credit they allowed, the wide range of their dealings, and their capital being mostly founded in landed property, which could not be rendered promptly available, the stability of the house was soon shaken, and at last overturned, and it ended in a bankruptcy as extensively ruinous as any speculation of the kind, perhaps, that has ever occurred in the country.

Another important factor was that the shareholders had little idea what was involved in banking. Alexander Ferguson, one of the directors, admitted that he 'had not knowledge or experience sufficient to enable him to judge what was the extent of credit that in prudence we ought to have given the country upon our then in paid capital'. A report in the *Scots Magazine* of 1772 noted of the Bank:

> Having only among them two or three young people, of merit indeed, but little experience in commercial affairs, the direction was composed almost totally of young gentlemen of the law, men, many of them of genius and spirit, but not conversant in matters of trade.

It was also argued that the Bank did much good in its short life. The loans offered for making improvements to landed property were instrumental in promoting drainage, planting and other cultivation improvements. New businesses were established, among them the Boghall Coal Works at Wallacetown. The same story could be told in Dumfriesshire, where 'some of the town improvement [in Dumfries] could not have been carried out and would scarcely have been undertaken' but for the Bank.

Robert Burns refers to the 'villainous bubble' of the Bank's life in a letter to his cousin, James Burness:

> Even in higher life, a couple of our Ayrshire Noblemen, and the major part of our Knights & squires, are all insolvent. A miserable job of a Douglas, Heron, & Co.'s Bank, which no doubt you have heard of, has undone numbers of them; and imitating English, and French, and other foreign luxuries & fopperies, has ruined as many more.

The Bank's finances proved to be troublesome to unravel, and the actions of some of its directors questionable. The famous writer, James Boswell of Auchinleck, composed verses entitled *On the Late Meeting of the Air Bank*, which were published in the *London Chronicle* of 30 December 1773:

> *Assembled now with equal truth we find,*
> *That all our schemes are **air**, and words are wind.*

The shareholders in the Bank lost their money, and many were forced to sell their lands to pay their debts. It has been estimated that £750,000 worth of property changed hands as a result of the crash. Among those forced into selling considerable portions, if not all, of their land were John Campbell of Wellwood, John Christian of Kinning Park, Archibald Craufurd of Ardmillan, Patrick Douglas of Cumnock, Robert Kennedy of Pinmore, Hugh Logan of that Ilk, David MacClure of Shawwood, George MacRae of Picton, and Sir John Whitefoord of Ballochmyle and Blairquhan. By August 1775 only 112 of the 226 partners were still solvent. Each shareholding in the Bank had cost £500, but at the collapse each partner owed between £2,200 and £2,600 per share.

The affairs of the Bank were not wound up until 1804. Some of the debt owed to the Bank could be reclaimed, but only over a lengthy period. Refunds of £60 were paid in 1807, £18 in 1811 and £20 in 1816. The Bank eventually paid off all its debts, at great expense to its shareholders.

The great Scottish economist, Adam Smith, even covered the Ayr Bank crash in his seminal work, *The Wealth of Nations*:

> In the midst of this clamour and distress, a new bank was established in Scotland for the express purpose of relieving the distress of the country. The design was generous; but the execution was imprudent, and the nature and causes of the distress which it meant to relieve were not, perhaps, well understood. This bank was more liberal than any other had ever been, both in granting cash accounts, and in discounting bills of exchange. With regard to the latter, it seems to have made scarce any distinction between real and circulating bills, but to have discounted all equally.

Despite the scale of the collapse, it did not signify the end of banking in the town. On 1 October 1773 James Hunter, merchant in the town, and a former cashier of the Ayr Bank, founded Hunters and Co. Two other Hunters were shareholders, as well as William Wood, James's son-in-law. The Bank only had £5,000 in capital and was very cautious as to whom it loaned money. Branches were opened at Maybole and Irvine. In 1821 Hunters and Co. purchased the Kilmarnock Banking Company, giving it a third branch. Hunters and Co. was itself taken over by the Union Bank of Scotland in 1843.

Quintin Kennedy founded the Ayrshire Banking Company in

1830. It grew to have nine branches until it sold out to the Western Bank in 1845. The Ayr Savings Bank was founded in 1909, later being amalgamated with the Savings Bank of Glasgow in 1933. It is gratifying to note that these institutions avoided the fate of the Ayr Bank.

11

THE BRIGS OF AYR

FIVE BRIDGES SPAN THE River Ayr within the town, if we do not count the structure at the bypass at Holmston. For many centuries there was but one, the Auld Brig, which is now such a famous historical landmark. It would probably not have survived the eighteenth century if it were not for Robert Burns making it famous as one of the subjects of his poem, *The Brigs of Ayr*.

Just how old the Auld Brig actually is has been the subject of debate for many years. King Alexander II granted a charter in favour of the burgesses of Ayr on 7 December 1236, in which he gifted the royal fishings of the rivers Ayr and Doon. This was to help pay 'for the maintenance of the bridge and the improvement of the harbour'. The bridge to which this refers to was probably a timber predecessor. Another early reference to the Auld Brig appears in the Burgh Court Book of 1440.

An old tradition in the town holds that the bridge was erected at the expense of two unmarried sisters surnamed Lowe. There used to be two carved faces, on the southern end of the bridge's eastern parapet, which were said to represent the sisters, but these have long since worn away.

In 1491 King James IV visited Ayr on a pilgrimage to Whithorn, but when he planned crossing the river found that the bridge was closed. The masons employed on the bridge at the time used a small boat to ferry him across. On arriving safely, and no doubt dry, at the other side, he gave the men a tip. The Exchequer Accounts of that year note the payment: 'Item, – the 17th November, to the massonis of the Bryg off Aire, ten shillings'. This is clear evidence that a stone bridge was in existence in the fifteenth century.

In 1588 the Burgh Council obtained permission from the crown to levy a toll on those who crossed the bridge, or a 'brig impost' as it was known. The money raised was required to repair the structure. During the repairs a turf dam was erected in the river to divert the water away from the buttresses whilst work was carried out. It is known that the turf used for this purpose was lifted from Newton Green. Behind the dam, any water which gathered was pumped out.

In 1782 a committee, appointed by Councillor John Ballantine, was set up to look into the condition of the Auld Brig. One of the members was Hugh Cairncross, who was described by the Scots architect, Robert Adam, as his 'man in Ayrshire'. They were not very confident of the Auld Brig's strength and made their first report to Ballantine on 4 April 1782:

> Having at your desire this day and formerly examined the situation of the Bridge of Ayr which for some time past has been supposed to be insufficient, we are of opinion that the pillar on which the second and third arches from the town rests is in a very dangerous situation, being rent in several places and the stones from the land flood mark as far down as we had an opportunity of observing much decayed and fallen out in many places. The third arch is fully worse than the pillar above described, being not only sunk and consequently partly separated from the pillars it rests on but rent in many places and the stones so much decayed that we are seriously of opinion it may give way in a very short time and without the least warning . . . a very precarious situation . . . [T]he smallness of the stones and their perishable nature [mean that the bridge is considerably weakened] . . . Hitherto we have not had an opportunity of examining the foundations but will as soon as the river is sufficiently low and report accordingly.

However, despite this unequivocal report, only minor repairs were carried out at that time.

When the New Bridge was opened the Auld Brig was relegated to a pedestrian crossing. However, by the late nineteenth century the condition of the older bridge had deteriorated so much that the Council considered demolishing it. Sir William Arrol, the famous engineer who had designed the Forth Bridge and who resided at Seafield House in Ayr, suggested that the bridge be demolished and replaced with a copy.

However, the citizens of Ayr refused to countenance its destruction and a committee was formed to raise the necessary funds to effect repairs. Members of the committee included the ex-Prime Minister, Lord Rosebery, and James Morris, a local architect, who wrote a book about the bridge. A public subscription was launched and donations solicited from interested parties. By 1907 the £10,000 required to restore the bridge had been raised and work began. On 29 July 1910, the fully restored bridge was handed over to the keeping of the Council.

A few memorial plaques adorn the bridge. One of these is inscribed:

> In admiration of Robert Burns and his immortal poem 'The Brigs of Ayr', this brig was, during 1907-10, restored by subscriptions received from all parts of the world. R.A. Oswald, Chairman of Preservation Committee.

At the centre of the bridge, on the upstream side, is a small sundial, often missed by the busy shoppers who tramp back and forth across the cobbles. Unfortunately the gnomon of the dial is broken, a long-standing consequence of vandalism. It is also questionable whether the dial would be of much use, as it is sur-mounted by a three-legged iron lamp stand, which must obscure many of the sun's rays.

At the northern end of the bridge is a railed-off area which contains a few remnants of a house. This is sometimes erroneously descibed as the Bridge Port, an old gateway that guarded entry to the town from the north, but it does at least occupy the site of the gatehouse. Whether any of the present masonry dates from the time of the Port is unknown. Near the Bridge Port close examination – and it needs to be very close – reveals a cobble that is inserted in the ground at right angles to the rest. According to tradition, this marks the limit of where market stalls could be sited.

There is a story that, about the year 1917, Captain J.C. Callaghan M.C., of the School of Aerial Fighting and Gunnery at Ayr Racecourse, flew his aeroplane beneath one of the Auld Brig's arches. Whether this actually took place has never been confirmed.

As previously mentioned, the Auld Brig was partially superseded when a New Bridge was erected. The present New Bridge in fact replaces the first New Bridge, which was destroyed in a storm. In 1784 a joint committee was established with the proposal of erecting a new bridge over the river. Its membership comprised many of the county's landed gentry, as well as Provost William Campbell of Ayr, Bailie David Limond, Dean of Guild John Ballantine and Councillor John Murdoch. However, the rest of the county was unwilling to supply funds to the burgh for the erection of a new bridge, so the Council determined to go it alone. In 1785 a petition was presented to parliament and in due course the bill was passed.

The original plan had been to replace the Auld Brig with a new crossing on the same site, but following an inspection by Hugh Gemmill, a mason and merchant in Glasgow, it was decided to build on a new site and leave the Auld Brig standing. This would also avoid the problem of having to supply a temporary ferry for the time there was no crossing.

Plans were obtained from Robert Adam, the architect famous for many local buildings, including Culzean Castle, as well as for 'Adam' fireplaces. He must have visited the town in 1785, for there survive signed drawings of unexecuted alterations to the Sandgate tolbooth from that year. An entry in the Bridge Accounts for 6 November 1788 records, 'To paid Robt. Adams, Architect, for Plan of Bridge, £31 10/-'. Adam's design incorporated five arches, the central one of which was higher than the rest. The parapets of the bridge were adorned with balusters and the buttresses had statues and the burgh arms on them. The work was started in May 1786 and completed in November 1788 at a cost of £4,000. Stone for the bridge was taken from the town's quarry, resulting in a complaint from James Wallace, tacksman of the Mills of Ayr, that Mill Street was badly damaged by the constant to-ing and fro-ing of horses and carts.

The keystone of the central arch, which was fifty feet wide, was laid on 20 August 1787. This resulted in 'an evening's jubilee of dancing, etc. among the artificers, as the undertaker was then relieved from the great anxiety occasioned the night before by the violence of rain and wind', according to the Reverend Stebbing Shaw, who was visiting the town from Hartshorn in England.

Alexander Stevens was the mason responsible for overseeing the work. He was a prolific architect, having in the previous forty years 'erected more stone bridges and other buildings in water than any man in these kingdoms'. Among his many excellent designs are the bridge over the Liffey at Dublin, and the locks and docks of the Grand Canal of Ireland. Numerous works executed by him can be found in the north of England and Scotland. The aqueduct over the River Lune at Lancaster is one of the greatest undertakings he was ever involved with, and, had he lived for a few months longer, he would have had the satisfaction of seeing it completed. He died in January 1796 at an advanced age.

At the same time Stevens was able to build for himself a rather fine town house, occupying a site on the south-east side of the bridge, in the newly created New Bridge Street. The Town Council minutes of 12 September 1787 record his petition for the right to build on the site, 'which house he meant to build in an elegant manner, which would lend ornament to the bridge', and with its grand double-bow front overlooking the river, it does just that.

The question of whether Adam's design was inadequate (many of his other bridges are still extant) or, alternatively, whether the local contractors did not build it to his specification has never been satisfactorily resolved. In any event, the first New Bridge lasted only ninety years. A storm and floods in 1877 damaged the bridge quite considerably, and the Auld Brig found itself pressed back into service. Fragments of the original New Bridge survive – the arms of the Burgh of Ayr are incorporated in a wall at the corner of Monument and Chapelpark Roads. Balusters from the parapets were used in the forecourt of the Pavilion, and the leaden statues of the classical deities Bacchus, Ceres, Mars and Pan were relocated to the gardens of Burns' Cottage and Monument.

The engineers Blyth and Cunningham designed the present New Bridge. This bridge has a flat roadway carried on five segmental arches. Like its predecessor, it has an open balustrade along the sides, and the quatrefoils are cut from granite. On the parapet is the date 1878: work commenced the previous year and the bridge was opened the following. It cost over £15,000 to build, and in 1881-2 required £2,000 worth of repairs. Twelve yards on the downstream side of the bridge are carved the letters AB on the riverside wall, indicating the upper limits of the jurisdiction of the port of Ayr.

Seen from the New Bridge are the remains of an old railway bridge which formerly crossed the river downstream from it. Standing on the west parapet and facing the harbour one can still see four sets of large round pillars in the river, now surrounded by rubble. These pillars formerly supported a railway siding that crossed from the north harbour to the southern quay. The bridge, which took a curved route, was erected in 1899 but with the decline of the harbour the rails were eventually lifted and the bridge demolished in 1978.

Heading upstream from the Auld Brig we are next able to cross the river on foot at Turner's Bridge. This is an iron footbridge that was opened in September 1900 at the expense of A.M. Turner. Plaques adorn the trelliswork, noting that J. and H.V. Eaglesham were the engineers responsible for the design and that William Clarke was the contractor. Eagleshams were well known architects and engineers in their day, and were responsible for many buildings in the town.

Turner owned Ayr and Newton Breweries, which was established in 1789. The brewery buildings were located at the southern end of the bridge and covered almost two acres. The business was greatly extended when Turner acquired it, so that it had 'ample stores, drying-kilns, boiling-coppers, coolers, etc. as well as the cask-washing and bottling departments'. Turner also made aerated waters. The brewery obtained its water from a four-inch borehole that was sunk 300 feet within the site, the artesian well being sufficient to supply its demands. Early advertisements note that, 'according to Analyst's Reports, these Springs are specially adapted for Brewing purposes, imparting a delicate flavour and fine aroma only found in High-Class Ales.' Turner was a councillor in Ayr for a time, and a Justice of the Peace.

Further upstream we come to the main railway bridge, originally known as the Water Bridge, to the downstream side of which is a cantilevered footpath, known locally as the Cagewalk, linking Smith Street with Riverside Place and Gordon Terrace. The railway bridge was erected in 1856 when the railway was extended from Ayr south to Stranraer, the section from Falkland Junction to Ayr Station being opened on 15 May 1856 for goods. It is twenty-six feet wide, and has four arches of sixty feet span.

The main ring road bypassing Ayr town centre crosses the river by Victoria Bridge, which was constructed in 1961 of concrete and steel and opened on 19 April by the Dean of Guild, Adam Hart. Consulting engineers were F.A. MacDonald and Partners, the bridge being the work of Motherwell Bridge and Engineering Company. A plaque at the bridge's northern end commemorates those responsible for its construction. The Victoria Bridge was widened in 1977. As the name implies, the bridge occupies the site of an earlier structure, erected in 1898 during Victoria's reign. At that time the bridge was twenty-two feet in length and thirty-eight feet wide. The bridge and approaches cost £8,000 to construct and it was opened on 26 April 1898 by the Countess of Eglinton.

A footbridge within Craigie Park allows walkers to cross the river from one side to the other. It was erected in 1974 and named the Craigholm Bridge. The last bridge across the river associated with the town is the Overmills Bridge, dating from 1963, which carries the bypass over the river, just below the site of the town's Over Mill.

12

DAVID CATHCART –
LORD ALLOWAY

IN THE OLD CHURCHYARD of Alloway is a large memorial erected over the grave of David Cathcart, Lord Alloway, who died in 1829. He was a prominent figure in Scottish history.

David Cathcart was born in Ayr on 28 December 1763, the son of Elias Cathcart and his second wife, Agnes Ferguson. Elias's first wife, Helen, was the daughter of Hew MacHutcheon, Provost of Ayr in 1703. Elias was a merchant in the town who imported tobacco from Virginia before the revolution, and wine from France. He was a bailie in 1745 and served as Provost of the burgh from 1757 until 1759. He founded the town's poor house. Cathcart's business was so successful that he purchased the lands of the Kirk Crofts and Nether Crofts at Alloway in 1754 and formed a small estate that he named Greenfield.

Elias Cathcart died in 1776 at the age of seventy-three. Although David was just thirteen years of age, he inherited the Greenfield estate and lived with his mother both there and at their other property, Gayfield House, which stood just outside Edinburgh. His mother died in 1816 at the age of eighty-one.

David Cathcart started his education at Ayr Burgh School and thereafter was a student at Edinburgh University. At the age of twenty-one he qualified as an Advocate at the Scottish Bar on 26 July 1785. He married Margaret Mure, daughter of Dr Robert Mure of Blairston and Brockloch estate in Maybole parish, in 1793. Margaret's brother died childless in Jamaica in 1794 whereupon she became heir to the estates. When her father died in December 1801 she inherited Blairston, which was also known as

Middle or Nether Auchendrane. Margaret was not to enjoy her inheritance for long, for she died at Edinburgh in 1802, leaving a family of six, four sons and two daughters. Elias Cathcart, the eldest son, became heir to his mother in the lands of Auchendrane when he came of age in 1819.

Cathcart was elevated to the bench as an ordinary Lord of Session on 8 June 1813, following the resignation of Sir William Honeyman, Bt. Lords of Session were entitled to take a title, and he adopted the name Lord Alloway. It was remarked that his elevation was a tribute to his remarkable ability, considering that a government he did not support – he was a keen supporter of the Whig party – had appointed him. Cathcart served as a Lord Ordinary for thirteen years, an unprecedented term in the judicial world. In order to avoid accusations of bias in his judgements, he no longer attended political meetings nor used his right to vote following his appointment as a judge.

Cathcart had a powerful intellect and a profound knowledge of the law, and he was, in consequence, in considerable demand. And yet he was noted for his modesty and integrity, which made his peers hold him in high esteem. He was 'greatly respected as a judge, [and] was not less so as a private gentleman', a contemporary noted. He regarded the more humdrum cases as just as important as the bigger ones, reasoning that they were of considerable significance to the litigants. In the initial stages of his career he experienced some opposition to his views, but as time passed he soon gained the respect of his peers. Cathcart's mother used to say that if her son 'performed his duty to his country as faithfully as he had done to his clients, she would have no reason to feel ashamed of his character'.

He owned some land near Wellington Square, which was known as Provost Shaw's Park. This was feued in the early nineteenth century and the streets built thereon named Alloway Place and Alloway Park. An open square, to be named Alloway Square, is shown on Wood's 1818 map of Ayr, but this was never built. Cathcart took great delight in making improvements to his lands, planting trees and improving the quality of the landscape. He made a number of improvements to Blairston House, which was an old fortified tower house. When not engaged in Edinburgh's courts, Lord Alloway spent much of his free time there.

On the resignation of Lord Hermand, Lord Alloway was elevated to the position Lord of Justiciary in 1826, taking his seat in the Second Division of Court. Among his many close acquaintances, Lord Alloway numbered Sir Walter Scott, who noted in his *Journal* that they attended a dinner at Oxenfoord Castle, near Edinburgh, on 5 July 1828, and returned to Edinburgh together.

Alloway was involved in many controversial and high profile cases. He sent Malcolm Gillespie to the scaffold in 1827. Gillespie was 'renowned as a most venturous excise officer', according to Sir Walter Scott, but had turned to forgery and was found guilty of twenty-seven charges of passing forged bills of exchange.

One of Lord Alloway's last cases was the most historic in his long and distinguished legal career. William Burke was brought before his court, charged with multiple murder and disposing of the bodies to the surgeons in the colleges of Edinburgh for dissection. His accomplice, William Hare, had turned King's Evidence to bring about a conviction. Burke was hanged, and attention now turned to Hare. Only two of the judges were of the opinion that Hare should be tried, Lords Alloway and Gillies. All the others followed the Lord Advocate's opinion.

Three months later, on Monday 27 April 1829, Lord Alloway died at his home of Blairston, or Auchendrane. The funeral, which took place on 4 May, was a large one, and the coffin was transported to Alloway Kirk where it was laid to rest within the confines of the ruined church. Elias Cathcart, his eldest son, succeeded to the estates, but sold off Brockloch in 1829 and Alloway or Greenfield in 1830. The remaining parts of Blairston he renamed Nether Auchendrane in 1830, reviving the original name.

13
RIDE IN RADICAL BLOOD!

IN THE EARLY NINETEENTH century interest in local politics grew significantly, and many Ayr residents came to resent the fact that control of the burgh was in the hands of an elite few. Put simply, the ordinary resident had no real say in the selection of councillors. The members of the town's Guild and Trade associations sent a resolution to the Council, requesting greater involvement in the choice of representatives. The Council, while claiming to be sympathetic to the resolution, did not act, arguing that though there might be 'mismanagement and neglect' in some other burghs, the business of government in Ayr was in good hands.

The residents of the town were none too happy with the lack of change, and in 1818 formed a Radical Association. Most of its members were shoemakers and weavers. For a short time a Radical newspaper, the *Ayr Chronicle*, was produced.

James Logan became the secretary of the Ayr Radical Committee, but he was a 'notorious rascal and spy' who informed the police of Radical movements. His release always followed suspiciously soon after each arrest. Bait was set in an attempt to trap unwitting Radicals. One Campbell of Townhead was a known Radical. A barrel full of gunpowder was left outside his house door and a watch put on it to see if he would succumb to the temptation and take it in for possible future use. Campbell, however, did not fall for this ruse. In fact, he completely ignored it and, after a few days, the bait was removed.

A demonstration was arranged to take place in Wallacetown in November 1819, to which other Ayrshire branches were invited. The meeting was held in a field belonging to the Cross Keys Inn, located in the Back Riggs, which lay between Wallace Street and

Limond's Wynd. Thousands were in attendance and the carnival atmosphere was boosted by the sound of pipe bands. Banners were held aloft and cheers erupted when the speakers proposed reform. Two troops of Ayrshire Yeomanry were sent to police the meeting, under the command of Colonel Alexander Boswell of Auchinleck (the same person who organised the memorial to Burns at Alloway). They stood at a distance with their swords unsheathed, but they did not require to take action. Boswell, who was the Conservative MP for Plympton in Devon, had been quoted as saying that he 'would ride in Radical blood up to his bridle reins!'

Boswell listened to the Radical delegate from Ayr, William Adam, who was a shoemaker from George Street in Wallacetown. After the speech was finished Boswell was heard to say that Adam was fit only for hanging, words which were repeated to the Radical. Realising that his life was in danger Adam disappeared from his home. Within a few days a warrant was issued for his arrest but, despite a twenty-four-hour guard on his home, he was never caught. Adam did not return to his house for a full year thereafter.

In the early spring of 1820 rumours abounded of an imminent Radical uprising. A general strike had been proposed to take effect from 1 April and it was rumoured that a local landowner was willing to lead the Radicals of Ayr in the uprising. This landowner was Richard Alexander Oswald of Auchincruive, a known proponent of reform. He was visited by two men who tried to convince him to become the commander of the newly formed Radical Army, mainly for his liberal opinions but also for his military experience, for he had been the commander of the Ayrshire Yeomanry before Boswell took over in 1816. Oswald refused, and persuaded the men that they should make themselves scarce. He then rode to Ayr where he made a statement to the Sheriff claiming that the Radicals were trying to implicate him. He also feared that government spies were trying to plot a charge of high treason against him.

Such was the fear of an uprising that the old army barracks in the town were reopened, manned by the 10th Hussars and 4th

Royal Veteran Battalion, the latter being four hundred strong. The Loyal Air Volunteers had been reformed in 1819 as part of the Ayrshire Yeomanry, under the command of Lieutenant-Colonel Alexander West Hamilton of Rozelle. He was succeeded by Major Dugald Campbell of Thornyflat, a veteran of the Peninsular Wars and Waterloo. The Yeomanry itself had gained the nickname 'the Dandies' from their blue coats, white trousers and Glengarry bonnets. They were in demand for keeping the peace throughout the county, appearing at demonstrations held in Kilmarnock, Stewarton, Mauchline and elsewhere.

As the first day of April approached, tensions mounted. The Town Guard patrolled the High Street and Sandgate to prevent threatened attacks on the banks. On Sunday 2 April a soldier from Hamilton galloped into the town to warn that the rising was underway in Lanarkshire. He brought the request that every available soldier should be sent to Glasgow. Most of the residents were in church, but the church bells were rung in mid-service as a warning and the congregations rushed home. The Hussars and Royal Veterans left the barracks to march to Glasgow, and the Ayrshire Yeomanry met in the Academy playground to prepare for policing the streets. The burgh magistrates conferred with Major Campbell of Thornyflat and it was agreed that the Yeomanry should guard the town and quell any rioting which might break out.

The first day of the proposed strike, Monday 3 April, came with great expectation. It turned out to be little more than talk, the *Air Advertiser* noting that 'a great part of the inhabitants of Air, and the other towns and villages in the county, did little else but stand in the streets and converse on the subject of the alarms.'

On Monday morning, three troops of the Ayrshire Yeomanry paraded in the Sandgate prior to being issued with ammunition. Word reached the town of a riotous assembly of Radicals at Stewarton, to which one troop was immediately dispatched. As they rode through the streets of Wallacetown women and boys threw stones, sods and empty bottles at them. The Radicals at Stewarton made themselves scarce before the Yeomanry arrived.

Two regiments of the Yeomanry were dispatched to Glasgow, under the command of Major Ferrier Hamilton. Major

Crawford's regiment was sent to Paisley. The troops in Glasgow were subjected to taunts and threats, as well as having objects thrown at them from first-floor windows.

The Home Secretary, Lord Sidmouth, writing to Alexander Boswell on 18 April, noted that 'The Yeomanry of Ayrshire have had a distinguishing part in crushing the incipient Rebellion but the Civil Authorities must be constantly vigilant and on the alert or tranquillity will not long be preserved.' Those Radicals who were arrested were tried before special treason courts that were set up by a Special Commissioner of Oyer and Terminer. The court for Ayr was held in the New Parish Church in Fort Street, opening on 4 July. Seventeen Radicals from all over the county were indicted. Only four turned up: John Dickie, weaver; Thomas MacKay, tailor; Hugh Wallace, weaver; and Andrew Wyllie, flesher. All were from Mauchline. The remaining men absconded, most of them fleeing the country. Francis, Lord Jeffrey, and Henry, Lord Cockburn, two celebrated Scots advocates, were selected to represent the prisoners. The Ayr firm of solicitors, Messrs Morton and Harper, acted as their agents.

The High Court of Justiciary was moved to Ayr in order to hear the pleas of the prisoners. It turned out that there was insufficient evidence to prove the charges, but the Special Commissioners were keen to convict at least one person. Thomas MacKay, who was a young lad, was advised to plead guilty to the charge of treason. He refused to do this, but the authorities, as well as his friends and family, who were supposed to have been influenced by the government, persuaded him that it would be in his best interest, and that he would receive a pardon later.

The trials were scheduled to commence on 29 July. When MacKay pled guilty in the New Church those present were astonished, especially his counsel, J.P. Grant. The trial reconvened on 9 August when Grant and E.D. Sandford represented the prisoners. MacKay still wished to plead guilty, thinking that he had struck a deal to get off. However, after the pleas had been given, the Lord Advocate informed the court that he did not wish to bring evidence against the other three, being of the opinion that one conviction would be enough to bring the rest of the county to its senses.

The Lord Justice Clerk then passed sentence on MacKay:

> That you be taken from thence to the place from whence you came, and that you be drawn on a hurdle to the place of execution, and there be hanged by the neck until you be dead, and that afterwards your head be severed from your body, and your body be divided in four quarters to be disposed of as His Majesty shall direct and may the God of all mercy have mercy upon your soul.

The sentence was not, in fact, carried out.

Two men were brought before the Ayr circuit court, charged with stealing guns. One was Joseph MacGhee, who was charged with taking a pistol from William Kerr of George Street, Content; the other was John Forran, who stole a pistol from William Logan, hardware merchant in Ayr. Both entered pleas of not guilty; MacGhee was found not guilty and acquitted, but Kerr was found guilty and sentenced by Lord Meadowbank to fourteen years' transportation.

Another man brought before the court was a young deserter from the Ayrshire Yeomanry. He had been marching with the soldiers across the Fenwick Moor when he decided that it would be 'better to be quaffing strong ale at his own fireside in Mill Vennel than fighting the Radicals at Hamilton or Strathaven, and run the risk of getting a hole knocked through his gullet by a Radical pike'.

The threat of civil war gradually subsided over the summer months and on 8 August most of the Ayrshire Yeomanry were stood down. A few remained in action, however, and were needed to disperse mobs in the town on occasion.

However, the rising was at least partially successful. In 1832, the Great Reform Bill was enacted which allowed those paying £10 or more in rates within towns to vote in elections. Despite many being sentenced to death, only three men in the whole of Scotland were actually hanged for their part in the affair – James Wilson of Glasgow, and John Baird and Andrew Hardie of Stirling. Known as the 'Political Martyrs', they were later commemorated by monuments.

14

THE IRON TYCOON – JAMES BAIRD

JAMES BAIRD, WHO BECAME a resident of Ayr, was one of the greatest entrepreneurs in Victorian Britain. He was born at Lochwood in Old Monkland parish, Lanarkshire, on 5 December 1802, one of seven brothers, the son of Alexander Baird and Janet Moffat. His father was a farmer who realised that his sons would have a greater chance of success if they moved into the coal and iron industries that were expanding rapidly at that time. Baird and his brothers established William Baird and Company and erected their first blast furnace in 1828, employing the newly developed hot-blast method. In 1844 he extended his business into Ayrshire when he purchased the Eglinton Ironworks at Kilwinning. Baird's business soon grew to considerable proportions. He was a hard taskmaster and strict employer, and totally opposed to trade unionism; during one industrial dispute he even had strikers arrested in their beds at one o'clock in the morning and immediately taken away for trial. On the other hand, he gave generous financial support to a host of worthy causes including schools, churches and hospitals.

Baird's fingers were in many pies. Among those businesses he held directorships in was the Forth and Clyde Canal Company, the Caledonian and Dumbarton Railway, the Clydesdale Railway, and the Glasgow, Bothwell, Hamilton and Coatbridge Railway. He was also on the board of the Western Bank.

Baird was a staunch Conservative. He contested the Falkirk seat at the election of February 1851 and narrowly defeated James Loch, infamous as the Duke of Sutherland's factor and perpetrator of the highland clearances. Although he held the seat until 1857, he was not a particularly enthusiastic MP and disliked speaking in the House of Commons, where some regarded him as a lower-class northern industrialist and disliked his abrasive manner.

He married late in life. His first wife was Charlotte Lockhart, whom he married in 1852. She died a few years later, and he married Isabella Hay in 1859. There were no children from either marriage.

In 1853 Baird purchased the house known as Craigwell from Lord Nigel Kennedy for £22,000. The mansion was too small for Baird, so he built a brand new Scottish baronial mansion, three times the size of the house it replaced. The new residence was named Cambusdoon House, and the farm of Greenfield was cleared to create ornamental policies around it. Cambusdoon was latterly a school, but was eventually demolished, though a few fragmentary remains can still be seen in the small park at Alloway.

Baird owned thousands of acres of land throughout Scotland. In 1872 he held 19,599 acres in Ayrshire alone, paying £8,043 in rates and £1,000 for minerals. In addition to Cambusdoon, he bought Auchendrane in 1862, Muirkirk in 1863 (costing £135,000), Drumellan in 1866 and Wellwood in 1873. He inherited the ancient seat of Auchmeddan in Aberdeenshire in 1856. The peninsula of Knoydart was acquired in 1857 at a cost of £90,000. Reflecting his status and power, Baird was appointed a Deputy Lieutenant for the county of Ayr in 1868. He had previously held that office in the county of Inverness.

In the middle of the nineteenth century plans were made to build a church in Alloway. The village had formerly been a parish in its own right, hence the Auld Kirk, but was joined to Ayr in 1690. Baird was a staunch adherent of the Kirk and in 1857 gifted funds with which the present building was erected. The architect was Campbell Douglas, and he designed a grand Gothic building constructed from pink and grey sandstone. Baird's wife Charlotte, who died later that year, laid the foundation stone. It cost £1,750 and was opened on 10 October 1858. The stained-glass windows in the church are particularly fine. In 1860 Alloway was once again created a separate parish.

However, the construction of the church caused a national out-cry against Baird. When the walls began to rise it was discovered that the building would obstruct the view of the Burns monument from Burns' Cottage. Robert Howie Smith, editor of the *Ayr Express*, stirred up the objections to such an extent that deputations from Burns Clubs from all over the world were sent to try and halt the construction, despite the fact that the people of Alloway had chosen the site. Baird's response was that 'The kirk's needit, and it will be biggit.' The editor of the Conservative *Ayr Observer*, the Reverend William Buchanan, took Baird's side in the matter, and after a while the furore subsided, as most people came to accept that the church did not desecrate the shrine of Burns.

Baird was a devoutly religious man, and gifted thousands of pounds to church projects. However, his gifts were not made lightly, as he would only enhance the efforts of others, and not gift cash outright. He despised fawning, and those begging for money were likely to be turned down. Many anecdotes are told of his generosity, but also of those who were disappointed in their approaches. A minister from a church near Kilmarnock once tried to get Baird to pay off his church's debt, and at the same time persuade him to fund a new manse. The minister did some preparation before paying Baird a visit. He discovered that the ironmaster enjoyed an early morning stroll and a smoke. The minister accordingly made his way to Cambusdoon early in the morning. Instead of arriving at the house in a carriage, he was let off at the gatehouse, from where he walked to the house. He was fortunate enough to meet Baird on his walk.

'Mr Baird, I presume?'

'Aye it is,' Baird replied. 'Wha are ye?'

'The Reverend A– B– , and I'm taking the liberty of calling on you on very special and important business. Whilst praying this morning for guidance during the day, and seeking help where only it can be found, and much requiring that help for my church and my poor flock, I seemed to be directed from on High to direct my steps towards Cambusdoon, where I would find relief from all my anxieties. In fact, Mr Baird, the Lord has sent me to you for the help I need.'

'Then the Lord's wrang this time; I'll gie ye nothing,' was Baird's reply, and nothing could persuade him to part with a penny for the minister's proposals.

James Baird, the iron and steel tycoon

By 1865 Baird employed 25,000 workers, mainly in Ayrshire and Lanarkshire. He was the owner of ironworks at Gartsherrie in Lanarkshire, in addition to those at Dalry, Hurlford, Kilwinning, Lugar and Muirkirk. To supply them Baird also owned and operated numerous coalmines and ironstone pits.

Baird was noted for talking in what was regarded as a rather rough Scots tongue, which was not liked by certain contemporary landowners. He had little time for people who put on airs and graces, and it is said that when the chairman of Ayr Water Company tried to purchase the Milton Springs in order to increase the burgh's water supply, his toffee-nosed attitude so annoyed Baird that he refused to help. The chairman, Hugh Cowan, along with civil engineer J.I. MacDerment, paid Baird a visit and asked for his assent for developing the Milton Springs. Baird refused, stating that the water supply available from the Springs could only cope with the demand for a few years or so. Instead, he suggested that the town should dam Loch Doon and pipe the water into the developing burgh. The men from the water company disagreed, convinced that their own proposal was best. The argument went on for some time, both sides sure of the other's folly. Eventually Cowan told Baird that they would use their power to take the supply from him, hoping that it would persuade Baird to climb down. This did not work, and the burgh needed an Act of Parliament to obtain the Springs. The Act cost £4,000, the Milton Springs themselves £5,000, and over £20,000 was needed to dam the site and lay in pipes. Within a few years it was discovered that Baird was right in his predictions that the Springs could not cope with the growing demand for water. By this time Loch Doon was no longer an option, and the burgh needed to dam Loch Finlas in 1887 and lay in an even longer pipeline to supply the town.

The people of Ayr disagreed with Baird's politics when he tried to offer support to the Conservative candidate. The crowd jeered him at hustings. When he tried to address the crowd, they yelled at him 'Dam the waater! Dam the waater!' As a result of this and other insults, Baird did not donate money to good causes in Ayr for many years. It is claimed that because of the attitude of the water company and of the Council to Baird, he abandoned plans to donate to the town a new Educational Institute, to be modelled on the highly successful Dollar Academy. The cost of the building itself was to be around £50,000, and a further £50,000 endowment was proposed to ensure its financial stability.

One of the few major projects that Baird was willing to support in Ayr was the construction of a wet dock. Plans for this had long been mooted, and it was to be sited at the Newton Loch. Provost Thomas Steele was given the job of approaching Baird for additional funds, the Council not trusting the job to anyone else. Steele was more successful in his negotiations – instead of getting help to build a dock worth £30,000 as proposed, Baird suggested constructing a bigger basin, and he was willing to advance £165,000 to assist in the excavation and construction of walls. The work began soon after, but the dock was incomplete at the time of Baird's death, and was not opened until 1878.

In his last few years James Baird gifted £500,000 to the Church of Scotland. He had been a Commissioner to the General Assembly on a number of occasions. He was instrumental in founding the trust that was to administer it in July 1873, and for a short time was able to help distribute it. As with all his gifts, the trust would only give to those who had raised funds or had put in a lot of work themselves. This money still supplies funds that are distributed by the Baird Trustees. The trust was founded 'with the view of helping to promote the spreading of the Gospel in connection with the Church of Scotland, endowing parishes, augmenting parishes, augmenting stipends, assisting students, and keeping up an annual Lecture'. One wit obviously believed he had ulterior motives and described his largesse as the greatest fire insurance premium ever paid!

James Baird died at Cambusdoon on 20 June 1876 and was buried in the small burial ground that lies to the back of Alloway church. Such was his prominence that the shops in Ayr, and in the other towns where he owned businesses, closed on the day of the funeral. The folk of Alloway erected a stained-glass window in Alloway church to his memory in 1877. At the time of his death his estate was valued at £1,190,868 14s 5d.

15
THE FOLLY BARON – JOHN MILLER

ONE OF THE MOST eccentric of Ayr's many colourful residents was John Watson Miller, better known as 'Baron' Miller. He was a keen supporter of development in the town and was responsible for rebuilding part of the town centre. He was described as 'a pawky Scot' and was undoubtedly the town's most picturesque figure, noted for his long white beard, and for carrying a stout cudgel wherever he went. His speech was described as slow and terse, but he was renowned for his optimism and sense of humour. He dressed in a simple manner, hiding his riches, and in his later years was described as being behind the times. He often walked from his home to the auction rooms in the town, where he liked to think of himself getting a bargain. His purchases were usually of a unique antiquarian nature, and his home at Fort Castle was filled with strange and obscure relics.

John Miller was born in November 1820 and brought up in the village of Catrine, thirteen miles east of Ayr. He was the nephew of 'The Bonnie Miss Miller', one of Robert Burns's 'Mauchline Belles'. The connection with Burns pleased Miller immensely, and he was a keen admirer of his works.

One of Miller's first known activities took place in 1832. At that time there were numerous marches in support of the Reform Bill, one of which set off from Catrine, heading for Sorn. Miller, who was just eleven years old, joined the marchers on their way, carrying a little green flag inscribed 'Down with the Lords'. He maintained allegiance to the Radical cause all his life, being a supporter of the Liberal Party, and often visiting the Liberal Club in the Sandgate. He is known to have worked behind the scenes in burgh politics for sixty years, but he would never agree to address a crowd. 'I am not adapted for public speaking,' he would respond when asked.

Miller was sent to Ayr to work as an apprentice for Mr MacCririck, gunsmith, a long-established firm in the town. Before completing his apprenticeship with MacCririck, Miller moved to Calcutta in the Indian state of Bengal, where he found employment with the famous gun-maker, Joe Manton. Manton and Co. supplied guns to the maharajas and to the many British residents of the country. Miller would often relate how India was at that time subject to innumerable corruptions and intrigues. He was keen on some of the Indian customs, and he is said to have had an affinity for the Buddhist religion. In India he befriended William Stewart of Gearholm, who was also to settle in Ayr.

In the spring of 1852, John Miller set sail from Calcutta and arrived back in Ayr. His business had been so successful that he was in the position of being able to afford substantial property. In 1852 the lands of Montgomeriestoun, which had been formed out of the citadel and immediate area, were put up for sale at auction. In 1663 these lands had been created a Burgh of Barony in an attempt at establishing a new village there, but this had failed.

The auction for the Barony of Montgomeriestoun took place in Edinburgh on 28 July 1852. A deputation was sent from Ayr with the intention of acquiring the lands for the Common Good fund. At the auction the reserve price was revealed and, as a result, no offer was made for the lands. The deputation, thinking it could negotiate a lower price with the Ailsa trustees, did not make one either. John Miller arrived too late for the auction, but on passing the auctioneer's office went in to enquire if the property had been sold. Discovering that it had not, he made an offer of £2,560 which was accepted. Miller, knowing that the lands formed a barony, immediately styled himself Baron Miller. He is known to have stated occasionally that he had as much right to style himself 'baron' as many of those in the House of Lords. The title deeds to the property were highly prized by Miller. Written on parchment, they had been signed by Charles II himself.

In the centre of the lands the old tower of the parish church, which had been taken over by Cromwell's men, was still standing. Miller engaged the Ayr architect John Murdoch to extend this tower to form what he named Fort Castle. This was a peculiar vertical building, with odd gothic windows, oriels, corbels and turrets. Inside the castle Miller amassed a veritable museum of oddities, collected over many years. Here could be seen Indian arrows, Chinese gongs, alabaster carvings, pianos, telescopes, carvings and ornamental weapons from the Far East, clocks, paintings, copper tuns from the old brewery, parts of wrecked ships and rocking horses.

A postcard featuring Fort Castle around 1905

Baron Miller liked to test his technical proficiency in a variety of fields, one of the most lasting being the turret at the corner of South Harbour Street and South Beach Road, perched precariously on one of the angles of Cromwell's fort walls. His own hands constructed this corbelled turret and he worked at it for some time. Although he was proud of the structure, it was noted that he rarely visited it after it was complete. Since that time, the turret has been known locally as 'Miller's Folly'.

This was not the only construction work he undertook on his own account. On one occasion he was dismantling the roof of an old building connected with the Fort Brewery when he fell to the ground. Though he was seriously injured with a number of broken ribs, the skill of Dr Naismith and Miller's strength saw him return to full health.

Within a short time of acquiring the lands, Miller engaged the architects Clarke and Bell to draw up a plan for new streets and housing. Feus were sold from as early as 1857 and the present streets of Eglinton Terrace, Eglinton Place, Montgomerie Terrace and Bruce Crescent were laid out, named mainly after the previous owners' titles. Within a few years what was previously sand dunes and grassy slopes had been converted into one of the town's most desirable residential areas.

John Miller had a skill in making fiddles that went beyond the ordinary. He devised and altered many of the mechanical tools needed to create them. He also adapted scientific apparatus to try and soften the sounds and accentuate the harmonics of various musical instruments.

Although a keen antiquarian, Miller did not always treat his historical artefacts with respect. On one occasion he excavated the ground surrounding Fort Castle in order to determine the floor plan of the ancient kirk of St John. Whilst digging, he found some of the original flagstones from the church. Rather than preserving them for what they were, Miller regarded them as suitable material for a new building. The stones were eventually incorporated in the altar of the Holy Trinity Church in Fullarton Street. A few ancient stones discovered by Miller were kept for display, including floral cross-slabs, other gravestones and carved pieces from St John's Church. Miller also acquired the carved roundels from the original Adam New Bridge of Ayr. Metal which had come from the bells of St John's was discovered by Miller and melted down. He used this to cast small handbells.

Miller was noted for his love of children. On one occasion a group of boys had trespassed onto his lands from the Academy, with the intention of having a good-going fight, away from the prying eyes of the teachers. Two lads engaged in fisticuffs, and the noise from the assembled crowd attracted Miller's attention. Instead of running out and bellowing at them to clear off, Miller approached the 'ring' quietly and made his way between the lads. In his slow manner he said, 'Away down to the shore, boys, and finish your fight there; you'll find the sand a grand easy place to bury your dead in.' One of the spectators recalled, 'I think his quiet manner impressed us. We perhaps felt just a little foolish, and we did not go to the shore.'

In the early years of the twentieth century Miller offered to sell to the Town Council the ground between Montgomerie and Eglinton Terraces for a public open space, but this was rejected. One of those who voted against it was Police Judge Smith who, though one of Miller's close friends, took a principled stand on the issue.

Miller died after a short illness at Fort Castle on Tuesday 21 June 1910, in his ninetieth year. By this time most of his lands had been developed, apart from the grounds immediately adjacent to the tower. He had offered to sell this to the burgh as a park, but they refused to buy it, perhaps still smarting at their failure to acquire it years before. In 1911 advertisements appeared offering it for sale at a cost of £2,700. The 4th Marquis of Bute acquired it in 1924, and took down Miller's castle leaving only the original tower still standing. This he restored to its original appearance.

Ayr's connection with Miller did not end when he died. As late as February 1950 his trustees, one of whom was N.R. Rowan of Poole in Dorset, offered the old fort walls that still belonged to the trust to Ayr Town Council.

16
THE ROADMAKERS

AYR HAS TWO UNIQUE connections with the surfacing of roads. The first, and most famous, is through John Loudon McAdam, who was born in the burgh's Sandgate on 21 September 1756, the youngest of a family of ten. His birthplace survives and is known today as Lady Cathcart's House. He was a son of the McAdams of Waterhead, at Carsphairn in Galloway. His father, James McAdam, founded the first bank in Ayr in 1763. His mother, Susannah Cochrane, was related to the heroic Grizel Cochrane and a cousin-german of the 8th Earl of Dundonald. John Loudon was the second son; the elder, James, became a captain in the army but died in 1763.

In 1760 the McAdam family moved to another house, off St John Street, and they also lived at Blairquhan Castle at Straiton, at which time young John attended Mr Doig's school in Maybole. Another family home was Lagwine Castle at Carsphairn, but this was destroyed by fire, following which the family moved to America. His father was active in business there, and on his death in 1770 young McAdam was sent to work with an uncle who was a merchant in New York. There he married Glorianna Margaretta Nicoll, daughter of a wealthy New York lawyer and businessman, in March 1778, and they had four sons and three daughters. When McAdam returned to Scotland at the close of the revolutionary war in June 1783, he rented Dumcrieff House near Moffat until 1784. At the age of twenty-seven, he was able to purchase the estate and mansion of Sauchrie, south of Alloway, for £3,000, which he owned for thirteen years. It is claimed that the first ever 'macadamised' road led from the Ayr – Maybole road to Sauchrie House.

In 1786 McAdam partnered the 9th Earl of Dundonald in the establishment of a tar works at Muirkirk, known as the British Coal Tar Company, but this proved to be less than successful. He had greater success with his work on the numerous turnpike trusts that he advised. McAdam had devised a method of building roads which was far superior to any previously used. It had long been thought that bigger stones and wider wheels were the answer to rutted roads, but McAdam turned conventional thinking on its head and experimented with small sharp stones, which could compress and bond together, and thin cartwheels which ran smoothly across them. Contrary to popular belief, McAdam never laid a tarred road in his life, the connection of his name with tar being confused with his Muirkirk works.

John McAdam was appointed a Deputy Lieutenant of Ayrshire, was a burgess of Ayr from 1789, and from 1793 to 1794 was a councillor in Ayr burgh. He was also the Major Commandant of the Ayrshire Militia Cavalry. In 1798 he moved to Falmouth following his appointment as superintendent of the victualling department of the western counties of England. In 1815, now living near Bristol, he was appointed General Surveyor of the Bristol roads, and there developed his road-building techniques further. By 1818 McAdam was a consulting surveyor to thirty-four road trusts all over Britain and in the following year published *A Practical Essay on the Scientific Repair and Preservation of Roads*. In 1820 he was granted a government pension of £4,000 for his work in improving the operation of the Post Office. Three years later he appeared before a select committee of the House of Commons to advise on the practicalities of replacing granite setts in the towns with macadam roads. As a result of his advice, the main streets in London, Edinburgh, Dublin and other major centres were macadamised, and his surname became accepted as a word in the English language. The House of Commons awarded him a grant of £10,000 in 1825, and in 1827 he was appointed General Surveyor of Roads for Great Britain.

Glorianna died in February 1825. Two years later McAdam married her cousin, Anne Charlotte De Lancey. He was offered a knighthood in 1834 but turned it down on account of his age (he was by then seventy-eight). Instead, his eldest son, William, having died, the honour was conferred on his second son, James Nicoll McAdam, who was General Surveyor of the turnpike roads in London.

McAdam died on 26 November 1836, 'without pain or even complaint for he died of old age after a useful, long and honourable life', according to his son. He was buried in the old churchyard of Moffat, as his dying wish was 'to sleep amidst the mountains of Moffat'. In 1936 a monument commemorating McAdam was erected in Ayr's Wellington Square by the Institution of Municipal and County Engineers.

The mixing of tar with McAdam's method of using angular stones is usually credited to E. Purnell Hooley of Nottinghamshire, but tar macadam was actually pioneered by another Ayrshire man, John Walker. His father, William Glassford Walker, was born on 16 February 1812 at Kilmaurs, the son of agricultural labourer, John Walker, and his wife, Janet Glassford. W.G. Walker was manager of the Kilmarnock Gas Company, and in 1872 set up in business for himself by purchasing Walter Stewart's chemical works in Ayr. He brought his family to Ayr where they lived at first in the Old Manse. He later lived in a house at 18 Midton Road, where he remained until his death.

W.G. Walker began tar distilling at a new chemical works, named Hawkhill Chemical Works, erected on a greenfield site at West Sanquhar Road. (This road was later renamed Somerset Road after the football and athletic ground known as Somerset Park.) The new works had a 120-foot chimney constructed in 1878, which was the tallest stack in Ayr at that time. The works were located south of the Glasgow and South Western Railway's Ayr and Mauchline branch, and from Blackhouse Junction a siding was constructed into the grounds of the works. On passing through the works gate, this siding split into two lines before merging again and stopping at buffers. At the point where there were two lines, a crane was positioned so that it could lift loads from the wagons. The residual products of various gas works were brought to the tar distillery, where tar was made by removing some lighter oils.

W.G. Walker soon expanded, with depots being established in Ayr, Edinburgh, Dundee, Glasgow and Belfast. Ayr was still the head office of the Company. Mastic asphalt roofing, flooring and tanking became the Company's main activity. The bulk of asphalt was at this time manufactured at the Edinburgh depot.

It was after his father's death in 1894 that John Walker devised a new method of surfacing roads and pavements using tar. This required tar to be laid over a base of virtually any material to leave a surface which was strong and dust-free, a vast improvement over other road surfaces, and one which was much cheaper than other permanent surfaces. The tar macadam was put down in three layers, leaving a period of time between each layer to allow the tar to 'bind'. The roadway into Walkers' works was laid in the new method, and after several months' use showed no signs of wear and tear. A writer in the *Ayrshire Post* of 26 October 1894 confirmed its success:

> After a trial of several months, and subjected to the severest traffic tests – loads of several tons making no impression thereon – it has to be pronounced . . . as most excellent. Its advantages over causeway, cement, asphalt, macadam, &c., are manifold. First and foremost, the cost is less than by another system; there is comparatively no noise from traffic over it; there is no dust or mud – a desideratum; it is a humane invention, in that there is an absence of concussion, and at the same time it gives a sure footing for horses; it is easily cleansed, and can be washed as clean as a model dairy floor in a few minutes; it is not affected by weather, and does not take on the frost to the same extent as other pavements; it can be laid in less than no time. . . . [T]he Town Council should encourage this home industry by laying Newmarket Street with this new pavement, and also the slopes at either end of the Auld Brig. . . . It is a pity that Messrs. W.G. Walker & Sons are so near home. Had they boomed from London, Newcastle, or Timbucktoo there would have been a scurry after this new pavement, and delegates would have been posted off to see its work. Truly a prophet is nothing in his own country.

Perhaps the writer of the above was unduly pessimistic, for in 1895 Walkers were invited to lay part of Gordon and Buchanan

Streets in Glasgow with their new tar macadam method. This contract was of great importance to the firm in order to achieve a wider recognition for their new method. However, it nearly came to grief, for the city fathers of Glasgow would not allow them to lay the tar in the three layers they had devised, insisting that it was to be laid in as short a period as possible, and in a single layer. This led to some acrimonious correspondence between the Council and the Company, which spilled over into the *Evening Citizen*. On the 26 November 1895 an article appeared in that paper under the title 'The Tar Macadam a Failure'. In the report it was stated that Mr Whyte, Master of Works for the city, was antagonistic to the new paving. He was quoted as saying that 'next to granite, wood has proved to be the best material for paving in Glasgow.' Messrs Walker were quick to respond, and a letter appeared in the *Citizen* of 2 December 1895, challenging the report:

> In the case of Buchanan and Gordon streets, which could not be closed against traffic unless between Saturday afternoon and Monday morning, we were compelled to depart from our usual method of laying our tar macadam composition for heavy traffic; while certain circumstances over which we had no control prevented us from completing the work satisfactorily at the time. Two attempts were made to remedy matters, but as the streets could not be closed for a few days they were unsuccessful. Further, we had difficulties to contend against which are apparently unavoidable in regard to city streets. A few days after it was laid Gordon-street was cut up by the Water Department, and Buchanan-street likewise passed through the same process by the Electric Lighting Department. These breakages, so soon after the composition was laid, certainly were very detrimental. The repairs referred to in your paragraph apply only to these breakages. Tar macadam may or may not be the solution of the street-paving problem, as you remarked in a leading article a few months ago; but our experience is that when it is laid by our usual method it has, next to granite, more resistance to the Scotch system of horse-shoeing than wood.

The *Ayrshire Post* writer called at Hawkhill to find out Walkers' side of the story. He found that Mr Whyte had prejudged the success or otherwise of the tar macadam, and had been very slow in granting Walkers a trial section of street, ultimately letting them lay a patch of Gordon Street and Buchanan Street. However, he refused to allow them the same conditions as other road surfacers and insisted that all the work be done on a Saturday afternoon! He also advised Walkers that the depth of material on Gordon Street to the concrete foundation was four inches, when in fact it was nearer six inches. Walkers, having sent up sufficient composition to lay four inches, had to make do with the material they had ready. Thus the roadway was not built to Walkers' usual specifications.

Nevertheless, the *Post's* writer noted that Walkers had 'laid their tar-macadam paving in nearly every town of importance in Scotland, and repeated and extended orders prove the entire satisfaction it is giving. There are ample evidences that as a street paving it is at present without an equal.' The writer also returned to Hawkhill and noted with satisfaction that 'since I last had the privilege of inspecting it, some sixteen months since, there is not the least perceptible sign of wear. It is as good as when first laid down. Nay, I believe it is firmer and more consolidated.' Walkers had in the intervening months made some improvements on their product, and developed a different method of top dressing the tar macadam. This gave the surface a skin, which made it impervious to weather and abuse. This new method was tried out in the yard of Ayr Gas Works, and the *Post* journalist noted that, despite being subjected to heavy traffic and roughshod horses, it showed no signs of failure. Over the years John Walker gifted to his home town pieces of ground in the Hawkhill district for the purpose of making improvements to the roads using his method.

Many local towns began resurfacing their main thoroughfares. Irvine Town Council considered laying 'Tar Macadam composite pavements' in 1895. The first roads there to be covered in tar macadam were laid in 1909. As a result of Walkers' success in winning orders to lay tar macadam in many of Scotland's towns, several new depots were opened.

Walkers continued their expansion into the new century. An advertisement from the *Ayr Directory* for 1909 gives details of their business. Included are tar macadam for roadways, footpaths, tennis courts and damp courses. 'Walker's Sanitary Rockbuilding Composition' was produced for floors, as a vertical and horizontal damp course. 'Limmer' rock asphalt was produced for roofs, floors, balconies, roadways and footpaths. 'Dachonite' roofing composition was supplied for flats roofs of all descriptions. The Company also supplied compressed natural rock asphalt slabs for street paving, with different thicknesses available according to traffic. Walkers also appealed to history to advertise the versatility of their product, noting that Noah used tar to waterproof the ark and that it was used in the construction of the Tower of Babel; the Egyptians used tar in the construction of the pyramids, in embalming the dead, and in the creation of reservoirs, and many ancient cities used asphalt as cement in construction work.

Lorry owned by W.G. Walker and Co. Ayr Ltd, with driver

John Walker lived in a house known as Windsor Villas, at 27 Miller Road, Ayr. This street was the first roadway in Ayr to be laid with tar macadam. He married Elizabeth Murdoch Donald and they had four children. Walker died in December 1930, in his eighty-first year, and was buried in Ayr's Holmston Cemetery. He left an estate worth £22,469.

Despite John Walker's innovation of 1894, credit for the invention of tar macadam has been given to E. Purnell Hooley, County Surveyor of Nottinghamshire at the turn of the century. The story is told that while on a visit to the Denby Iron Works in Derbyshire in 1901 he noticed that a barrel of tar had burst and that the contents had seeped over a roadway comprised of slag from the furnaces. The area where the tar had spilled was hard-wearing and dust-free. Hooley decided to copy it, and set up his own company to produce tarred roads. The company was named Tar Macadam (Purnell Hooley's Patent) Syndicate Limited, and a number of roads were laid in this manner. The company experienced financial difficulties early on, and had to be rescued. It was renamed Tarmac Limited and as such continues to this day.

On the death of John Walker, W.G. Walker and Sons' registered office moved to Parkhead, Glasgow, and the Hawkhill Works was now classed as a branch office. John Strathearn Walker, son of John, was one of the directors. In 1938 the Company was registered anew in Edinburgh under the name of W.G. Walker and Co. (Ayr) Ltd, of Hawkhill Works, Ayr. John Strathearn Walker died in 1959.

On 14 April 1940 the chimney at the Hawkhill Works was demolished. Although the stack was originally part of Walker's chemical works, this part had been sold to James Dickie and Co. two years earlier. The *Ayrshire Post* of 19 April that year reports the passing of a local landmark:

> When the tall chimney stalk in the Hawkhill Works was brought down by steeplejacks on Saturday afternoon one of the best known landmarks in the Hawkhill district disappeared for ever. The felling operation was carried out during the Ayr – Kilmarnock match, and although the site of the chimney is within view of Somerset Park, few of the spectators saw the chimney fall. The chimney was built in 1878 and at that time was the highest in the town.

It is possible that few of the Ayr spectators witnessed the collapse of the chimney due to the fact that Ayr were beaten three goals to two by Kilmarnock!

W.G. Walker and Company (Ayr) Ltd continues to operate from the Hawkhill depot. The Walker family no longer have any connection with the firm, which is now owned by the Thomson family. The firm specialises in all aspects of roofing work, metal fabrication as well as high-pressure drain cleaning and maintenance.

17
SHIPBUILDING

AYR WAS AT ONE time an important shipbuilding centre. The building of boats has been recorded in parish records for centuries. A charter issued by Alexander II in 1236 granted the five pennylands of Alloway, Corton and Carcluie to the burgesses of Ayr for a rent of £10 per annum, on condition that they did not use growing wood from the lands, save for what they required for their own houses or building their own ships. The exchequer rolls for the period also confirm that the burgh was an important shipbuilding centre. In 1263 William, Earl of Menteith and Sheriff of Ayr, claimed a refund of £60 15s 8d for the cost of making ships for the King, plus 7 merks for the cutting and shaping of 200 oars.

During the late eighteenth and early nineteenth centuries the ships were built with timber most of which would have been grown locally, but oak was imported from England and Wales, and fir from Danzig. A number of sawpits and sawmills existed for the conversion of timber into suitable planks. Most of the old shipyards were on the north side of the river, with some accounts claiming that there were five different yards. In 1791, fifty men were recorded as being employed in shipbuilding at Newton, earning from 20 to 22 pence per day. The business was at that time estimated to be worth £5,000 per annum. By the beginning of the nineteenth century there were approximately two hundred men employed in shipbuilding in Newton parish, a number which declined over the next thirty years. By the late 1820s it was reckoned that only four or five men found employment in repair work.

John Fraser built ships at Ayr in the latter half of the eighteenth century. One of his vessels was the *Buck*, a sloop with a displacement of fifty tons, constructed for Ayr wine merchants, Oliphant and Co., in 1767.

Wood's 1818 map of Ayr shows two building yards at the southern end of Newton Green. One of these is named Connel's [*sic*] Building Yard, Charles Connell and Co. also having a timber yard further upstream. A plan of the harbour produced in 1827 shows shipbuilding yards in the same area. Wooden-hulled vessels were built on the Newton side of the harbour for the tobacco trades in the late eighteenth century.

The firm of Ralston, Smith and Company was one of the longest-established builders at Newton. The Company was taken over by Hugh Cowan and renamed Cowan and Sloan. Business picked up following the sale, and the Company was noted for the slip that it used to haul boats out of the water, constructed in 1831 to the plans of Thomas Morton, who had invented the patent slip in 1819. Over the following six years the yard was responsible for repairing 111 vessels. In the same period nine new ships were constructed, varying in size from 47 to 433 tons. Between forty and fifty builders were employed, earning between 18 shillings and £1 for working eight hours in the winter and ten in the summer.

Between 1830 and *c*.1860, when the yard closed, Cowan and Sloan, and Sloan and Gemmel as the business became, built over twenty ships. Sloan and Gemmel were famous for building sailing clippers, some of which were renowned for their speed. The *Tamerlane*, built in 1834 with a capacity of 427 tons, at one time held the record for sailing between Britain and the East Indies. Another barque, the *Oriental*, was also noted for its speed. A number of schooners built by the Company were used in the coastal trade with Liverpool. These included the *Eglinton, Gazelle* and *Katinka*. The Company also built the yacht *Tammie Norrie* for the Marquis of Ailsa; it was 41 feet long, 12 feet 3 inches broad and had a hold 6 feet 4 inches deep, and rigged as a smack it could carry 27 tons.

One of the most famous schooners ever to be launched from Sloan and Gemmel's yard was the *Felix*. This 110-ton schooner was completed in 1850 for the Arctic explorer, Sir John Ross (1777-1856). Ross often journeyed to Ayr from his home at the

North West Castle in Stranraer to supervise the construction. In the year the *Felix* was launched, with a crew of former whale-fishers, Ross led an expedition to search for Sir John Franklin, who had left on an Arctic expedition five years earlier and had never been seen again. Unsuccessful in this, Ross returned to Britain in 1851, and was appointed a Rear Admiral.

With the arrival of steel hulls the older shipbuilding yards lost trade and most were forced to close. Sloan and Gemmel's yard was sold to D. and A. Fullarton around 1863. Fullarton was responsible for the 163-ton brigantine *Zeolite*, launched in 1863. The *Guyana* was among the six other vessels built in the yard. After Fullarton, the Ayr Shipbuilding Company operated the yard until 1877 when the lease expired and the harbour commissioners closed the yard.

In June 1881 Ayr Harbour Trustees decided to construct a new shipbuilding yard on the south side of the river, to adjoin the newly constructed slip dock that had been built by James Young of Edinburgh. The slip was built on a north-south axis and was crossed by a pedestrian swing bridge. The yard covered an area of approximately four and a half acres. A guidebook of 1894 describes the facilities the yard offered:

> A large brick building [contains] the workshops, machinery, and other appliances for the carrying on of the construction department. Here may be found a splendid outfit of woodworking machinery of every kind, hydraulic cranes for the lifting of heavy materials, and all the special machines and apparatus which are required in a shipyard. Power is obtained from a very large and well-built engine, which drives the machinery and an endless number of lathes, drills, planing machines, saws, and other tools. The shipyard does not possess what are known as dry docks, but has an excellent and a well-constructed patent slip, which admits of the convenient handling of vessels of very large tonnage. Throughout the entire premises the works are equipped with the most modern conveniences and shipbuilding appliances, and the whole establishment presents an example of thorough organisation, which speaks well for the sound practical experience and ability of its management.

MacKnight, MacCredie and Company took on the new yard in 1883. Alexander MacCredie was a boat-builder from the

Maidens, but he left the partnership in 1884 and returned there. The business then became known as Samuel MacKnight and Company. Within ten years the yard employed six hundred men. The Managing Director was a Mr Scott who later moved to Ireland and set up the Dublin Dockyard Company.

MacKnight was responsible for a considerable number of ships. Between 1883 and 1902 the yard had built sixty-five vessels of varying sizes. The first ship completed was the 237-ton steamer *Elagh Hall*, built for J. Christy. Great were the celebrations at the launch on 13 September 1883. Four vessels were completed in 1884, including the *Kyle* which was built for Ayr Harbour Commissioners in 1885.

The *Madge Wildfire*, a 210-ton passenger steamer was launched on 17 June 1886. The ship was 190 feet in length, 20 feet at its widest. Powered by an engine supplied by Hutson and Corbett, the steamer was capable of carrying 983 passengers at speeds up to sixteen knots. The *Madge Wildfire* served in the Clyde for almost forty years, carrying passengers to the Holy Loch, Rothesay, Millport and other resorts. The ship was renamed twice, requisitioned for duty in both world wars, and ultimately broken for scrap at Troon in 1945.

Four ships were constructed in 1888, from the small 75-ton *Tigh-na-Mara* to the huge 1,329-ton *Dunmore* for the Dunedin Steam Shipping Company. In 1890 a pair of vessels, the *Gascony* and *Guienne*, were built for the Moss Steam Shipping Company of Liverpool, each having a displacement of 1,134 tons.

The *Lady Rowena*, a 332-ton steamer, was launched in 1891. This vessel was 200 feet long and powered by a Hutson and Corbett engine. Built for the North British Steam Packet Company, it plied between the Clyde and Arrochar, until it was scrapped in 1923. The *Britannia* was launched in 1896, a sister ship to the *Westward Ho!* (launched 1892), both of which were built for P. and A. Campbell and Co. The largest ship built by MacKnight was the *Lord Aberdeen*, launched in 1889, with a capacity of 1,360 tons, and built for J. and A. Wyllie.

Samuel MacKnight died in 1897. His trustees continued to operate the yard until 1902, when the shipyard was taken over by the Ailsa Shipbuilding Company of Troon. From this time until 1929, a further 144 vessels were built at the yard. Ailsa Shipbuilding Company also specialised in paddle-steamers and coasters. On many occasions the hulls were launched at Ayr before being towed to Troon where they were fitted out with their engines. The Company's peak occurred at the time of the First World War, but during the depression which followed business was harder to come by.

One of the largest ships built at Ayr was ordered soon after the Ailsa proprietors took over. The *Hunterfield* was built in 1903 for the Lovart Steam Ship Company of Bo'ness. By 1907 smaller ships were in demand, resulting in a number of barges being laid out. These had a gross tonnage of only 45 tons. Eighteen were launched in 1907, and forty-three in the following nine years.

HARBOUR, AYR.

Ayr Harbour in 1913

By 1914 prospects for the industry were much brighter. In that year the 1,304-ton coaster *Maple* was launched for the Laird Line. Also constructed in that year was the 1,332-ton *Seamew* for the General Steam Navigation Company, and the 1,580-ton *Nantes*. During the war a number of ships were built and, in the years that immediately followed, the largest ship launched at Ayr came down the slip. This was the *Drake*, a 1,597-ton vessel for the General Steam Navigation Company.

The steamship *Ailsa II* was launched in 1924, a smallish vessel of 120 tons which plied between Girvan and Ailsa Craig. The hull was 95 feet long and a Hall and Company engine supplied the power. This ship was renamed the *Lady Ailsa* before being sold to France in 1932.

The third-last ship to be built at Ayr was the *Ville de Papeete*, launched on 15 November 1928 for a French shipping company. The penultimate vessel was the *Cobargo*, launched in 1929 for the Illawarra and South Coast Steam Navigation Company, with a displacement of 860 tons. The last vessel launched was the *Durdham*, a 477-ton sand-dredger destined for the Bristol Channel.

Ayr shipyard was laid up in 1930 and no more ships were built there. The yard had been a casualty of the national rationalisation scheme that took place as a consequence of the depression. In December 1939 the Ailsa yard was reopened for a time. It was used for repair work to vessels required for naval service. When, in August 1943, the Admiralty proposed returning the yard to its previous owners, a deputation of shipyard workers petitioned the Council to save it. However, their pleas went unheeded and with the closure of the yard shipbuilding finally came to an end in the burgh.

The Ayr shipyard was acquired by the Ayr Engineering and Construction Company, which was a subsidiary of the London Graving Dock Company. The firm used the yard for the repair of small vessels, as well as some conversion work. The Company eventually closed the yard and, in 1971, Associated British Ports sold the site to Ayr Town Council. The slip was filled in, and blocks of flats currently occupy the site.

18
THIRTY YEARS OF THE TRAMS

PROPOSALS FOR INTRODUCING A tram service in Ayr were long in the planning. Ayr and District Tramways Company was formed in 1883. The Company raised capital with the intention of laying tramlines on which horse-drawn trams would be hauled, but the proposals were not considered viable and eventually had to be abandoned.

The Burgh Council opened an electricity generating-station in 1898, which made the possibility of electricity-driven vehicles a reality. An English company came to the town with proposals to start a service, but by this time the Council was keen to set up its own service. And so in 1899, when the Ayr Burgh Act was passed, it included powers allowing the Council to set up and run an electric tram service.

The Council's Tramways Committee was formed in 1900 and began to organise the creation of a tramway infrastructure. J.E. Winslow, a noted tramway engineer, planned the route, though his initial suggestion that the route should go down Miller Road and along the Esplanade before branching to Seafield and the race-course was not adopted by the Council. The work commenced in February 1901, and seven and a half months later the service was ready to go. Major Fred Coutts, who had previously been an engi-neer with Dundee Tramways, was employed as manager. A staff of thirty-five were employed under him – twelve drivers, twelve con-ductors, an engineer, a storeman, a traffic inspector, a night motor inspector, two clerkesses, four cleaners and an apprentice electrical engineer. A special meeting of the Council took place on 13 May 1901 at which it was proposed to establish the running arrange-ments of the business. The first uniforms were described as being similar to those worn in Dundee, no doubt due to Coutts's influence, but these were later changed to uniforms more akin to Glasgow's.

One of the resolutions passed at the meeting was the decision to operate the trams on a Sunday. When word of this spread through the town, there was an immediate outcry. Ministers fulminated against the proposal, and for months angry letters were despatched to local newspapers. Twenty ministers from the parishes of Ayr, Newton upon Ayr, St Leonards, Wallacetown and Prestwick signed a petition asking for the decision to be overturned. A second petition of residents received almost seven thousand signatures, and a further eight hundred were obtained in Prestwick. After a series of Council meetings it was agreed that the cars should run on the Sabbath for six months, after which a referendum would be held. When this took place on 26 April 1902, the ratepayers voted 1,252 for retaining the Sunday cars, 433 against.

On Thursday 26 September 1901 the burgh was proud to inaugurate the first half of the new service. The town was in carnival mood. The Council had purchased ten tramcars, five of which were paraded in convoy from the depot to the St Leonards terminus. Provost Thomas Templeton rode in Car No. 5, which headed the procession, halting for a while outside the Town Hall. The tramlines had been laid in the streets from Prestwick Cross in the north, heading south along Prestwick Road towards Main Street, across the New Bridge and a sharp turning to the left into the High Street.

The lines continued eastward then south towards the terminus at St Leonards, a distance of four miles. The lines were laid with a gauge of four feet eight and a half inches, and a large depot was erected at Bellesleyhill. Within a large shed three lines were laid side by side. A second shed with another three sidings was opened in 1902. A third shed was erected in 1923 on the north side of the road, in which four sidings were created, which could accommodate sixteen cars, and it also housed a paint shop.

Poles were used in the town centre to support the electric cables, but as these were located in the middle of the road they caused problems for traffic flow. Within a few years improvements were made with the erection of iron brackets and cable supports mounted on adjacent buildings. Electricity to power the trams came from the burgh's recently opened generating works in Mill Street.

Hurst Nelson of Motherwell built the tramcars. The first ten cars were open-topped double-decker vehicles, but single-deck trams were later added. The livery chosen was a deep maroon colour, embellished with gold lining. Two British Thomson Houston motors, producing twenty horsepower, powered the cars. Seating was provided for twenty-two on the lower deck, the upper deck having a further thirty-five seats, the bases of which tipped up like cinema seats to prevent them from getting wet in the rain.

An extension was made to the tramline on 1 June 1902, leading from St Leonards south towards Alloway. This allowed visitors to the town to visit Burns' Cottage and other attractions at Alloway more easily. The additional line meant that more tramcars were required, and six more cars were bought from Hurst Nelson. These entered service in May 1902 and seated fifty-nine passengers. At the end of the tram service's first full year it had carried 3,201,586 passengers.

Indeed, the trams were so popular that in 1904 a Confirmation Act of Parliament was required to permit the laying of a second track on the section from Bellesleyhill to the Grammar School. On the remaining stretches of single track a total of thirteen passing loops were made. A show car was added to the fleet in the same year, numbered 18, which was embellished with stained-glass windows on the lower floor, and a brass-railed upper deck. The car had been built by Hurst Nelson in 1902 for the tramway exhibition in London and was luxuriously finished to let the public see just how sumptuous trams could be. This car was used for special events, often being dressed in garlands and ribbons and paraded through the town. It made an appearance at the Coronation of 1911, after which time the locals referred to it as the 'Coronation Car'. When the Duke and Duchess of York visited Ayr to lay the foundation stone of the County Buildings in July 1931 the car was specially decorated.

William Grant was appointed General Manager in 1905,

when Major Coutts moved on to Paisley trams. Grant was to remain for the next twenty-five years. During his time as manager he issued every member of staff with a rules and regulations book that detailed how the service was to be operated. This detailed the maximum speed, which varied along the route, the maximum allowed between the Town Hall and Kirk Port being eight miles per hour. On Prestwick Road ten miles per hour was permissible whereas in the narrow section of the High Street at the Wallace Tower the speed was limited to four miles per hour. Many other rules were in force. For example:

> Motormen must not run over sticks, wire or other obstructions on the line as these are liable to get entangled with the motors and gearing. Stop the car and remove them.

In 1913 the tram company opened a branch line which went via George Street and Whitletts Road towards the new racecourse, which had been opened the year previously. The number of employees increased to forty-three in 1911. In 1907 a further two trams were acquired, two more in 1913, and another pair in 1915, bringing the total to twenty-four. One of these was a water sprinkler, later adapted for grinding the tramlines, and having a snow-plough attachment.

Opening of the Ayr Tram Service in 1901

A single-decker tram on the Ayr Racecourse Line

End of the line: 1932

Alterations to the track were made over the years. The Chief Engineer of Glasgow tramways inspected the whole set-up and made a number of recommendations. The ornate poles, which held up the electric cables, were removed and stronger steel poles were erected. In the busier sections, as in the centre of town, the poles were removed altogether, to be replaced by cables supported from nearby buildings, a boon to the other traffic in the street. All the points were replaced and the rails welded together.

In 1919 a loop was added at Alloway Church to allow trams to pass each other. In 1922-3 the track between the Grammar School and St Leonard's Church was doubled. At the same time the track from the depot to Prestwick Toll was doubled. Four more tramcars were obtained, this time second-hand, from Manchester Corporation. These cars were originally trailer cars on the Oldham, Ashton and Hyde service, but were converted to powered trams. Single-decked, they had seating for twenty-six. The drivers knew these cars as 'Mousetraps' from their tight cabins that prevented tall men from standing upright. They were also operated single-handedly, and were used on the quieter Hawkhill branch.

A number of employees became well known in the business. Tommy MacMillan was one of the Company's characters, operating single-handedly one of the cars that took spectators to the races. Alfred Sommerville was renowned for his engineering skill, and maintained the cars with loving care.

Ayr trams ran with some success for about twenty years, but as the rolling stock and rails began to age the Company started to lose money. In 1925 things became so bad that the Council had little option but to cut the employees' wages and reduce their working hours from forty-eight to forty-four per week. In response to these reductions the workers went on strike.

The largest number of passengers carried by the service was recorded in 1928, when 5,743,663 fee-paying customers were served. In that year a final two cars were acquired, again second-hand, from Dumbarton Burgh and County Tramways Company, which had closed. The last five years of the service proved to be unprofitable. In 1928 more money was invested in the service in an attempt to bring it up to date and, it was hoped, back into profit. In the winter of 1930-1 the track from the Town Hall to the Grammar School was relaid at a cost of £12,000. Some of the cars were modernised by fitting new motors and upholstery, making the journey considerably quicker and more comfortable.

On 11 August 1930 the councillors heard from Thomas Galloway, burgh treasurer, that the tramways were no longer profitable, and thus a drain on the public purse. He proposed that a vote be held 'of the ratepayers of Ayr as to whether they desire the tramway undertaking to be continued or not'. The vote did not take place, however, for the Council followed other plans. By this time competition from the bus companies was fierce and in 1931 it was agreed to sell the business to the Scottish Motor Traction Company. The business was sold for £19,000 plus an annual payment of £1,500 until 1 January 1953. The SMT promptly closed the tramway and replaced the service with buses.

The last tram ran on the lines on New Year's Eve in 1931. Car number 23 left Burns' Monument at 11.25pm and made the journey north to the depot. It was packed with travellers keen to savour their last 'hurl'. The conductor wore a black armband as a mark of respect for the service, and at the depot Driver Gibb, who had driven the very first car in 1901, was given the honour of shuttling the tram into the shed.

A fleet of twenty 32-seat buses replaced the tram service, charging the same fares – ordinary fares, work-people's fares, children's fares and half-crown seven-day tickets. One of the problems in transition was that the thirty male conductors who had operated the trams, needed for their strength in changing the connection to the electric wires, had to be replaced by women, paid at 6½ d per hour. When the service was fully operational thirty-two drivers and thirty-two conductresses were employed.

Most of the trams were scrapped in March 1932. Two of them were sold to South Shields and saw service there until the end of the Second World War. One of the cars, number 23, stood for a while in the manse garden of St James's Church. The depots at Bellesleyhill were sold in 1952 and used for other purposes. One building partially survives within a furniture store; the other is now a food store. Virtually all evidence of the tramway in Ayr has now disappeared, apart from an odd bracket that supported the cables still bolted to the first-floor façade of certain buildings in the High Street.

19
SUFFRAGETTES

EVER SINCE THE Great Reform Act of 1832, women had been agitating for the right to vote. One of the first major events in the campaign was the presentation of a petition to the House of Commons in 1866, but this was ignored. Soon things began to get more heated, and by 1867 a number of suffrage societies had been formed. Campaigning went on for many years, but finding that they were getting nowhere, some turned to more drastic means of bringing attention to the cause. Arson was one of the most common methods used. Many pillar-boxes were set alight and, in time, larger acts of destruction were perpetrated.

In December 1872 a group of Ayr men who supported the cause paid a visit to E.H.J. Crawfurd, MP. One of them was James MacDonald, the rector of Ayr Academy. Though he listened to the case intently, Crawfurd responded by saying that he did not agree with the enfranchisement of women. Despite this and other setbacks, the campaign continued, and petitions were organised nationally on an annual basis, to be sent to the Commons, and one came from Ayr in 1878.

However, there were those in the town who were not content with peaceful protest. Just after midnight on the night of Friday 4 April 1913, two miners were walking back to Ayr from the pit at Annbank when they spotted what they thought were flames within the stand of Ayr New Racecourse, home of the Western Meeting Club. Unsure as to whether there was a fire, they reported the matter to Mr Clark, a builder who lived nearby. He thought that the glow was the reflection from a furnace at a local works, but on investigating the site he discovered that the stand was indeed alight. The racecourse caretaker, Mr Findlay, was quickly summoned and the fire brigade and police sent for. The local water supply was insufficient, and the flames had taken such a hold on the building that their attempts at dowsing it were futile. Instead all their energies were directed at preventing the fire from spreading to the nearby trainers' and jockeys' quarters. The club stand was completely gutted, adding up to £2,000 worth of damage. On the following day a complete search of the building was undertaken, and lying amidst the wreckage were discovered a union flag and half-burned copies of *The Suffragette* and *Votes for Women*. It was also noted that the door had been forced open. That the fire was the work of suffragettes was confirmed on Monday evening at a meeting of the Women's Social and Political Union in London. In her speech Miss Annie Kenney stated that the government 'could no more put out the fire in their hearts than they could put out the fire on the Ayr Racecourse'.

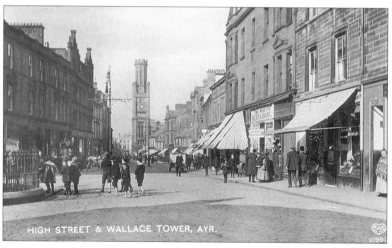

HIGH STREET & WALLACE TOWER, AYR.

The High Street in the early years of the twentieth century, when the suffragette campaigns were at their most intense

On 8 July 1914 an attempt was made by two women to set fire to Burns' Cottage. At around half-past two in the morning the watchman, Robert Wyllie, made a tour of the cottage, which he had been employed to guard for the previous fifteen months in case of such an attempt. He was sitting inside the cottage when he heard a thud outside. As he went out the back door, he noticed two women stooping down between two of the windows, depositing two containers in the gutter at the base of the building. As he rushed towards them they ran towards the garden fence. He managed to catch one of them, but the other scrambled over the fence. Pinning the woman to the ground, Wyllie called for assistance. He was heard by the neighbouring nurseryman, Mr A.H. Scott, and also by the keeper of the cottage, William Monaghan. They held the woman whilst Wyllie summoned the local policeman. Local residents who were awakened hurled insults at the woman, who kept up a nonchalant air throughout, remarking that it was a pity that she did not have a revolver with her. She was taken to Charlotte Street Police Station where she was held in a cell.

During interrogation the woman refused to name either herself or her accomplice. At length she gave her name as Janet Arthur, but this was found to be false – her real name was Frances (or Fanny) Parker, and it was discovered that she was a niece of Lord Kitchener. Two women constables searched her, not without a violent struggle. She was wearing a waterproof coat and a man's tweed cap; under this she wore a pair of trousers, into which her petticoats were tucked, and stockings over her boots to deaden her footsteps.

A police search of the Alloway area by car and cycle failed to locate the second woman. The villagers were roused from their beds at half-past three in the morning to assist, but no one was found, and Wyllie had no description of the woman to give. In Doonholm Road a bicycle was discovered, along with a quantity of brown wrapping paper, in which the canisters had been concealed. It was conjectured that the second woman had escaped on her own bicycle.

In a search of the cottage, at the spot where Wyllie first noticed the women, two bombs were discovered. They were biscuit tins covered in felt, each containing between eight and nine pounds of blasting powder. Around the casings was fixed a twenty-foot long fuse, which would have allowed a long period between ignition and explosion.

Fanny Parker was taken to the sheriff court where she was to appear before Sheriff-Substitute Broun. As she left the police station, a small group of women shouted 'They should hang her' and 'She should be shot.' Outside the court was gathered a large and hostile crowd, incensed that the cottage of their local hero had been so close to destruction. In court, Parker refused to enter the dock. Two policemen forced her into her seat, but the Sheriff-Substitute was unable to extract a declaration from her. She claimed that the court had no jurisdiction over her, and quoted lines from Burns's *Scots Wha Hae*. She yelled, 'You Scotsmen used to be proud of Bruce! Now you have taken to torturing women!' She claimed that prison warders at Perth did things to the women that they were ashamed to do in the open. Also in court at the time was a woman found guilty of receiving stolen goods who was due either to pay a fine of £1, or else face ten days imprisonment. Unable to pay, she was distressed at the prospect of a spell behind bars, but Parker arranged her fine to be paid from the funds in her possession at the time of arrest, and the woman was released. Fanny Parker was returned to gaol pending further inquiry, the crowds outside again jeering at her.

Fanny Parker went on hunger strike for five days in Ayr Prison. It was thought that due to her weakening state she would be released, but instead she was secretly transferred by rail to Perth Prison, where she was forcibly fed, a wardress slapping her face in the process. Doctors and wardresses then held her down for two hours to prevent her from vomiting. On her third day, Parker lost consciousness during force-feeding. Later in the same day she claimed to have been fed through the rectum, a process repeated on the next day. According to Parker's account, published in *Votes for Women* on 7 August 1914:

> One of [the three wardresses] said that if I did not resist she would send the others away and do what she had come to do as gently and decently as possible. I consented. This was another attempt to feed me by the rectum, and was done in a cruel way, causing me great pain. She returned some time later and said she had 'something else' to do. I took it to be another attempt to feed me in the same way, but it proved to be a grosser and more indecent outrage, which could have been done for no other purpose than to torture. It was followed by soreness that lasted for several days.

Fanny Parker was released from Perth Prison on 16 July. Still an untried prisoner, she was sent to a nursing home in Glasgow, from which she escaped before her case was due to be heard in the High Court in Glasgow on 27 August.

The second woman responsible for the Burns' Cottage incident is thought to have been Ethel Moorhead, an artist, but there is no proof of this. In her *Autobiography*, Helen Crawfurd claimed that *Mary* Moorhead, an Irish artist, was the second person, though no other reference to a suffragette of this name is known.

The final acts of suffragette arson in Scotland took place in mid-July 1914, with the Rosslyn Chapel explosion and an attempted burning of a new school building in Lanark.

Many public meetings were organised by the Women's Social and Political Union (WSPU) all over Scotland, to which everyone was invited, though the audiences consisted mainly of women. A typical example of one of these meetings was held in Ayr Town Hall on 20 May 1913. Although there were a number of policemen on duty within the hall, there were no 'scenes' of any description during the meeting, according to the *Ayr Advertiser*. A Girvan minister, the Reverend F. Carlisle Burton presided, and the two principal speakers were Mrs Kineton Parkes, secretary of the Women's Tax Resistance League, and a Miss Jarvis, of London. The Reverend Burton began the meeting with a short history of the suffragette movement, noting that

> it was felt, and keenly felt by a vast multitude of their leading ladies throughout the British Isles, that justice was not being done by the Imperial Parliament to the demands of the nation, and more and more this vast multitude of self-denying and self-sacrificing ladies felt that real justice never would be done until ladies had equal rights with men in Parliamentary representation.

Mrs Parkes addressed the meeting with the following resolution:

> That this meeting upholds the action of taxpaying women in refusing to pay all Imperial taxes until they have the Parliamentary vote, and calls upon the Government to introduce a measure granting to them the same control over national expenditure as male taxpayers possess.

She went on to explain that the Liberal government had coined the phrase 'Taxation and Representation go together,' but now that the women were saying this the government did not want to know. She blamed the government for the militant action of some suffragists, and added that 'Militancy was a perfectly natural state of affairs; there was nothing abnormal or freakish about it.' Mrs Parkes stated that tax evasion by women was the finest form of militancy, and that they would only pay Imperial taxes when they received the right to vote. They were happy to pay local rates because they had the municipal vote.

Miss Jarvis was reported as saying that:

> She firmly believed the fight for votes for women was going to be the biggest fight in history. They would not get the vote from any party unless they convinced them that they were going to have it at any price either to the nation or to themselves. They were prepared to pay that price and they were prepared to go just so far as might be necessary to win the vote. They were going to fight this matter right out, and the sooner the nation realised that the sooner would they once more become law-abiding citizens.

She referred to a recent raid on the headquarters of the WSPU in which an attempt was made to stop production of *The Suffragette*, and thus control the right to free speech: 'If they succeeded in that their militancy would be more, in excess of anything they had imagined, and the destruction of property would become enormous all over the country.'

The many suffragist meetings held throughout the country caused problems for the authorities in a variety of ways. At a meeting of the suffragists in Ayr, on Tuesday 29 May 1913, a number of men were brought down from Glasgow to act as stewards. They were members of the Dock Labourers' Union and, although most behaved impeccably, one Arnott Lockhart was charged with using obscene language in the town's Kyle Street and with assaulting two policemen who were taking him back to the station. He was fined £3 and his friend, John Paton, was fined £2 for obstructing and molesting the police.

Typical of the discussions taking place at the time was that of the Ayr Established Presbytery on 3 December 1913. A letter had been received from the Northern Men's Federation for Women's Suffrage, asking the Presbytery to support their movement. The Clerk put forward the resolution:

> The Presbytery receive the communication from the Northern Men's Federation for Women's Suffrage, and while dissociating themselves as a Presbytery from questions of party politics, they desire to express their deep sense of the grave social and moral evils against which the movement for women's suffrage is mainly directed; their thankfulness for the beneficent influence of women in the affairs of the Church and of the community; their sympathy with the desire for greater power to promote moral purity and social reform which political enfranchisement would confer upon them; their recognition of the justice of the claim that women's point of view should be represented in the government of the nation; and their earnest hope that by the co-operation of Christian men and women the evils referred to may be overcome, and the social, moral, and religious condition of their nation raised to a higher level.

An amendment was proposed by the Reverend J.C. Higgins, that the words about political enfranchisement and the justice of the women's claim to representation should be deleted. The Moderator of the Presbytery countered, 'If women had a vote in municipal matters and educational matters, both of which they had used with advantage, and if they paid their taxes and bore a share in the burdens of the empire, they had a right to the same recognition that has been extended to men in the past.' However, when put to the vote, Mr Higgins's amendment was carried by nineteen votes to eleven.

Not everyone was supportive of the suffragists. The Scottish League for Opposing Women's Suffrage (SLOWS) produced a small newsletter letting its members know of various meetings held throughout the country. Principal adherents of the league were Violet, Duchess of Montrose, and Sir John Stirling-Maxwell, 10th Baronet of Pollok House. The SLOWS had fourteen branches by 1914, one of which was in Ayr. This branch was typical in its organisation, holding regular meetings to which national figures in the anti-suffrage movement were invited to address the audience.

A large crowd gathered in Ayr Town Hall on 13 November 1913 under the auspices of the SLOWS. The principal speaker was Ethel Colquhoun of London, who was well known in literary circles. Local laird, Richard A. Oswald of Auchincruive, occupied the chair, and the platform party consisted of many other notables, including Dorothea, Countess of Glasgow, Mrs Arthur, Sir Charles Craufurd of Annbank, and Colonel Arthur C.F. Vincent. Mrs Colquhoun's address had the title, 'Why women should not have the vote.'

On 17 February 1914 the Ayr branch met in the River Street Hall to listen to Mrs Harold Norris from London. Ex-Bailie Wallace Allan was in the chair, and his views were given first:

> Their friends, who were pushing this [suffrage] movement, had very often misrepresented those who were not with them. It would take all night, he thought, to overtake the misrepresentations that had been made on the suffragist platforms, but there was one to which he would specially like to refer, and that was the insinuation that they were all opposed to women getting Parliamentary franchise and taking their part in party politics, because they wished to keep women in subjection. The anti-suffragists believed that it was not adding to woman's worth, to her usefulness, or to her womanly dignity to take part in party politics. It was not the case that they wished to keep women in subjection. . . . In the interests of the family and in the interests of the State they thought it was not for women to come into party politics, and were out to oppose the suffrage movement, which had been carried out with very much lawlessness. They were out to oppose the movement which for years now had greatly undermined freedom of speech, a precious heritage. They were out to oppose the movement which had molested men in our political life, in the Cabinet, in Parliament, and in the country, and the suffragists told them now that they had revolvers and meant to use them. This latest development to the present agitation was to take the form of something akin to murder. He defied anyone to justify militancy. He had never yet heard from any platform, or read in any periodical, any justification of militancy. The militant movement was simply premeditated, cold-blooded planning of criminality.

The suffragettes brought their campaign of violence to an end on the outbreak of the First World War. As a gesture of goodwill, the government introduced an amnesty and released the prisoners connected to the suffragist cause. The war years changed the country's attitude to women and, on the resumption of peace, the Electoral Reform Act was passed in 1918, granting the right to vote to women of thirty years and over. Further concessions were made in 1928 when Parliament gave all women over the age of twenty-one the right to vote. This gave them political parity with men, and the campaigning ceased.

20

THE SPORT OF KINGS –
HORSE-RACING IN AYR

HORSE-RACING AND AYR have been synonymous for centuries. The present racecourse in Whitletts Road is the leading venue in Scotland for both flat racing and National Hunt and, along with elite tracks such as Epsom, Newmarket and Ascot, is classified as a Grade One course. Many top-class meetings are held each year, with pride of place going to the Scottish Grand National, normally held in April, and the Ayr Gold Cup, run in September. In all, there are more than twenty days of racing each year and spectators enjoy facilities which rival the best on offer anywhere in Britain.

There is some doubt as to the exact date when racing in the town began. The eminent historian of the turf, John Fairfax-Blakeborough, notes that the earliest record of a race meeting was in 1576. This involved Lord Cassillis and his friends attending a horse race in Ayr during which a quarrel broke out over the starting procedure. A fight duly ensued, and it ended with John Kennedy of Penquhiren being shot through the leg and a John Crawford being shot in the thigh.

As the years passed racing became better organised, and much less hazardous for its adherents. In May 1609 the records of Ayr Burgh reveal that two gentlemen, the Master of London and a German nobleman, the Earl of Swissenberg, were entertained at a Golden Bell horse race run in the town. Racing was later given official recognition in 1698 when the magistrates of Ayr voted a sum of between six and seven pounds sterling for a Silver Dirk to be run for on the sands. Although the contest was held in August, this event is considered the precursor of the Ayr Gold Cup.

While racing on Ayr beach had its merits, there were obviously many drawbacks, and a decision was made in the late eighteenth century to hold the races at a more suitable venue. In 1770 what is now known as the Old Racecourse was formed on the town's Common at the instigation of a committee which included the Earl of Eglinton, the Earl of Cassillis and Mr Kennedy of Dunure. The course extended to sixty-three acres, and was rented from the Council at four times its agricultural value. The first officially recognised race took place in 1777 ('official' in that it is recorded in Weatherby's Racing Calendar). In 1788 the Council built a stone wall around the course, to a design by the architect Alexander Stevens, who was supervising the construction of the New Bridge at the same time. The course more or less followed this perimeter wall, with space for only a few spectators between the wall and the rope marking the edge of the racecourse. The shape of the field meant that the course was rather square, with sharp corners, resulting in a number of accidents when the horses took the bends at speed.

A grandstand, or 'View House' as it was originally known, was erected in 1787 on the lands of Seafield Farm, which lay on the opposite side of the road from the course. Entry to this viewing platform was restricted to the county aristocracy. Further viewing was available from the upper deck of a temporary structure that was removed at the end of the season. Admission to the upper floor cost one shilling, a not inconsiderable sum in those days. The lower floor of this building contained a refreshment room, one that was classed as far superior to the temporary marquees and tents which traders erected. The races also attracted sideshows and fairground rides, as well as farmers selling local produce. Spectators enjoyed eating kippers, most of which were supplied by the fishermen of Newton upon Ayr. The facilities at the old course were quite sparse: they were limited to a wooden hut where the horses could be saddled and weighed in, and a small paddock forty yards square where the horses gathered before the race began.

An advertisement of October 1775 for the 'Noblemen and Gentlemen's Purse' to be run for over the Ayr Course reads as follows:

On Tuesday, 10th of October, a Purse of Fifty Pounds sterling by any horse, mare or gelding, the best of three fair mile heats, and carrying the following weight:- Four-year-old, 8 stone; five-year-old, 9 stone; six-year-old, 9 stone 10 lb.; aged horses, 10 stone. And on Thursday, 12th of October, another Purse of Fifty Pounds sterling by any horse, mare or gelding carrying weight as above, the best of three fair mile heats. The horses to be entered on the Saturday preceding the races, when proper certificates of their age must be produced, and the enterer of each horse to pay Two Guineas of Entry-Money and five shillings sterling to the C.C. And if entered after the day, which may be done at the post to pay double. Three horses or mares belonging to different proprietors to start, or no race, and in that case Five Guineas to be paid for each of those entered. The Stewards and Judges appointed by them to be sole judges to determine all difference or dispute in or about the races.

William MacDowall, Esq., Castle Semple, and Hamilton Blair, Esq., of Blair, Stewards.

While there was racing all over the county, much of it was disorganised and frequently degenerated into strife and violence. However, Ayr was quickly to become the leading centre for well-organised meetings governed by proper rules. The credit for this must go to the Caledonian Hunt Club, which was formed in the late 1770s by a group of wealthy patrons. The Hunt raised Scottish racing to a new level by fixing the distance of races and the weights carried, and by organising annual meetings. Fortunately for Ayr, the town was one of the venues it selected for its meetings, and so every few years the Hunt staged a race-week in the town. Robert Burns was an enthusiastic supporter and, in 1787, dedicated a new edition of his poems to the Caledonian Hunt Club, which returned the compliment by generously subscribing for one hundred copies of the book. Many individual members of the Club were also to become patrons and supporters of the Bard.

Racing in Ayr went from strength to strength. In 1824 the Western Meeting was formed by the gentry of Ayrshire, Renfrewshire and Wigtownshire. Each member was obliged to make a contribution of three guineas to promote and develop racing and to observe the rules of the meeting. The Western Meeting was held annually in September and quickly became the leading event in Scottish racing. It was certainly the most eagerly anticipated social event of the year. For the 'quality' the week was a whirl of fashion parades, grand balls and theatre outings. Those further down the social spectrum did not miss out; side-shows and exhibitions of every description stretched from the Wallace Tower to the harbour. The races also attracted many patrons from outside the county. In 1835 Glaswegians travelled from the Broomielaw by sea for meetings and, from 1840, made the journey by rail.

There were many great characters associated with the sport in those early days. One was the Earl of Glasgow, renowned as a breeder of horses with stamina. Described by contemporaries as the 'Peppery Peer' because of his quick temper, the Earl once laid out a booking-clerk at a railway station in the north of England after a minor altercation. Another incident in England sheds further light on the eccentric peer's character: the Black Swan Inn in York issued him with a bill which read: 'Chop a shilling, champagne ten shillings, and for breaking waiter's arm five pounds'. Another colourful Ayr Turfite was the 'Tournament' Earl of Eglinton. In 1831 he won the Ayr Plate with the mare Bathsheba, the first top-class horse he ever owned. He also achieved great success in the classics, winning the St Leger with Blue Bonnet in 1842, and the Derby in both 1849 and 1850 with Flying Dutchman and Voltigeur respectively.

By the turn of the century it was clear the races had outgrown the Old Racecourse and, in 1904, the lands of Blackhouse and Braehead were acquired to develop a state-of-the-art venue. A new left-handed course of one mile four furlongs was laid out along with impressive stands and related facilities. Then, as now, Ayr Racecourse has rightly been considered one of the top courses in the country, and its management has consistently made strenuous efforts to keep the course up to the standard of England's top venues. In 1919 Western House was built to provide a clubhouse for the Western Meeting Club. In 1950 separate courses for flat racing, hurdle races and steeplechases were laid out and, in the same year, the first National Hunt meeting was staged. A further wave of improvements took place in the 1960s: of particular importance was the construction of the Eglinton Rooms in 1967 at a cost of £190,000; the pillared function room above the entrance is a notable feature on Whitletts Road.

The Ayr Gold Cup, the race that is so closely associated with the town, was first run in 1804. As Fairfax-Blakeborough points out it has been, since its inception, the classic of Scotland and as important to Ayr as the Grand National to Aintree or the Derby to Epsom. Beginning as an event run over a distance of two miles, the race was originally confined to horses trained in Scotland. The first winner was Chancellor, who repeated the feat in the following year. The race was reclassified as a handicap in 1855 when, to everyone's surprise, the horse which was first past the post, Lerrywheut, was disqualified because the jockey dismounted before returning to the winner's enclosure. The race was awarded to John Dory. In 1908 it became a six-furlong sprint, and it is now the richest race run in Scotland with prize money in excess of £100,000.

There have been many notable Gold Cups. In 1872 the great jockey, Fred Archer, then aged only fifteen, rode the French horse Alaric to victory by a margin of ten lengths. In 1936, Albert 'Midge' Richardson won on Marmaduke Jinks carrying only six stones thirteen pounds, the lowest winning weight recorded that century. Be Friendly, a horse owned by the great racing commentator Peter O'Sullevan, beat thirty-two other contenders to win the race in 1967, while, in 1992, Lochsong completed the unprecedented treble of Stewards Cup, Portland Handicap and Ayr Gold Cup. Many leading trainers are also associated with the race, none more so than the legendary Sir Jack Jarvis, who trained nine classic winners including two horses which took the greatest prize in racing, the Epsom Derby. Jarvis was arguably the most successful figure associated with Ayr races: he was not only the winning jockey on Kilglass in the 1905 Gold Cup but also trained three winners of the race, in 1937, 1938 and 1946. In addition, he trained an astonishing total of 103 winners at the Western Meeting, many of them for Lord Rosebery.

However, the most popular winner, at least with the people of

Ayr, was the giant horse Roman Warrior who won in 1975 ridden by Johnny Seagrave, at the relatively short price for the race of 8–1. The main reason for its popularity was quite simple: the horse was trained locally, by Nigel Angus, at Cree Lodge stables in Craigie Road. On the eve of the race there was some doubt as to whether Roman Warrior would even get a run. The going was expected to be soft, and this would not have suited the horse's action. However, a drying wind turned the soft ground into good and he took his place in the line-up. In a tremendously exciting contest Roman Warrior won by a short head, carrying a record weight for the race. There was great jubilation in the stands: indeed, the *Ayrshire Post* noted, 'The cheers that greeted Roman Warrior's win would have done justice to an Ayr United goal in the Scottish Cup Final.'

Ayr Racecourse in 2000

The other great race staged at Ayr is the Scottish Grand National. Originally run at Bogside in Irvine, it has long been Scotland's most prestigious jump race. The race transferred to Ayr in 1966, when the first winner was African Patrol, ridden by Johnny Leech. The Fossa won the following year, as part of a sequence of eighty races he would complete without a single fall. There have been many other notable winners over the years: in 1978 King Con, the 33–1 outsider from the small Scottish yard of George Renilson, triumphed; in 1981 Astral Charmer delighted the bookies by becoming the highest-ever priced winner at 66–1; while Androma, trained by Jimmy Fitzgerald, won two years in a row, in 1984 and 1985. There was a very popular winner in 2000 when Paris Pike the 5–1 joint favourite, owned by Major Ivan Straker, a former chairman of the Western Meeting Club, was piloted home by jockey Adrian Maguire.

None, however, is better known than Red Rum, perhaps the most loved racehorse of all time. Although remembered as an Aintree specialist, Red Rum had a great liking for Ayr Racecourse. He first competed at the course in 1972, finishing fifth to Quick Reply in the Scottish Grand National. In season 1972/3 Red Rum was being specially prepared for the Grand National and was sent to Ayr as part of his build-up, where he won a race by six lengths. A few months later, he took the greatest prize of all, the Grand National at Aintree. Following a second Grand National victory in 1974, Red Rum lined up three weeks later for the Scottish Grand National at Ayr. The great horse recorded another triumph, as he became the only horse ever to win the Aintree and Scottish Grand Nationals in the same season. In the quest for an unprecedented third Aintree victory, Red Rum also won the Joan McKay Chase at Ayr in season 1974/5, and proceeded to finish second in the Grand National in the spring of 1975. Given his outstanding record at Ayr it is entirely fitting that the course authorities commissioned a bronze statue of Red Rum jumping a fence. The statue now has pride of place next to the parade ring.

Ayr also has the distinction of being the only course outside England to host one of the five classics. In 1989 Doncaster Racecourse was unable to stage the St Leger, the last classic of the racing season. The race was transferred to Ayr and, as part of the traditional September meeting, 15,000 spectators saw jockey Steve Cauthen create racing history when winning on Michelozzo, the 6–4 favourite. The success of the race showed that Ayr has the facilities and traditions to host events of this stature. In fact, the course has gone from strength to strength in terms of spectator comfort. The Craigie and Princess Royal Stands have luxurious private suites and dining areas for corporate entertaining. The Club Stand has an impressive range of facilities including a Seafood and Champagne Bar, a Club Bar and the Chancellor Bar, named after the first winner of the Gold Cup. It is also possible to hire private marquees, which can accommodate up to twelve hundred people. In addition, the course has Western House which acts as the clubhouse for both annual and day members and offers restaurant and bar facilities. Given these top-class facilities, it is clear that Ayr Racecourse will enjoy even greater success in the future.

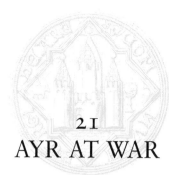

21
AYR AT WAR

PRIME MINISTER NEVILLE CHAMBERLAIN announced the declaration of war with Germany on Sunday 3 September 1939, at 11.15am. At the beginning of hostilities civilians were advised to carry their gas masks. Black-outs were ordered at night, and within weeks of the rules being introduced a few offenders were fined in the county court in Ayr. The townspeople could keep up to date with the happenings in Europe by attending war commentaries from the Ministry of Information, shown in the Odeon cinema in Burns' Statue Square.

One of the first effects of war experienced by the citizens of Ayr was the arrival at the railway station of four thousand children evacuated from Glasgow. The threat of air raids was regarded as so serious that thousands of city dwellers were sent to live in rural areas. The children were gathered at Ayr ice rink before being allocated 'billets', where they were to live for the foreseeable future. Soon, however, there were rumblings about the poor standards of discipline displayed by the children, as well as their lack of material possessions. It was reported that the children came wearing 'not what we call clothes in the burgh of Ayr', according to P.A. Thomson, the Town Clerk and chief reception officer. Various forms of entertainment were organised. The Popplewells planned putting on a matinee performance as a Christmas treat for the evacuees, but after a few months it was realised that the threat of attack from the air was less likely than at first imagined, and most evacuees had returned to their homes by December. Some children remained, and in January 1940 350 evacuees were taken to a concert in the Town Hall. The City of Glasgow sent £80 to help cover the cost, and the children were fed with a steak-pie meal, and after the entertainment was finished they were given an apple and an orange as they left the building.

Other rules were relaxed. A ten o'clock curfew, which was imposed at the start of the war, was quickly repealed, allowing the Gaiety Theatre and the town's cinemas to reopen. Of longer duration was the order to black out lights, which was designed to prevent enemy aircraft from spotting towns from the air at night. The lack of lighting was blamed for the death of Thomas Knox, aged forty-four, who was knocked down by a van in Beresford Terrace in January 1940.

Call-up papers were issued to a number of men, and conscription first took place in July 1940. More men were called to serve in the forces as the weeks passed. They were instructed to report to the Carrick Street halls for a medical before being allocated a regiment or unit. Only those with recognised conscientious objections, those employed in reserved occupations, and the medically unfit were not accepted.

Fund-raising for the war effort took many forms. The 'Penny-a-week' fund in aid of the Red Cross was resumed, having operated successfully during the Great War. The Women's Voluntary Services established a comforts depot in November 1939 and collected socks, mittens, mufflers, gloves, helmets and other items which were sent to the troops to make their lives slightly more bearable. Another means of supporting the war effort was to invest money in the government through the South Ayrshire Local Savings Committee. In 1942 a waste-paper drive was organised.

Public open spaces were put to good use during the war years. Cattle grazed on the local golf courses and most public gardens were converted into vegetable plots, as was one of the Belleisle courses, in the 'Dig for Victory' campaign. The Scottish Women's Land Army was reformed and underwent some training at Auchincruive College.

Ayr beach played its part in the war effort, with thousands of sandbags filled from it. Many large buildings had bags built up against them, acting as buttresses to give them extra support. Windows were taped with crosses to reduce damage and injury from shattering glass. In 1941 a mobile canteen was purchased for

Ayr and, in November 1942, the local MP, Sir Thomas Moore, opened the town's British Restaurant, one of a chain of government-run eating places, where decent meals could be had at a reasonable cost, for example, a three-course meal for one shilling.

Many large country and semi-rural mansions were requisitioned for the war effort. Among those used were Craigie and Belleisle houses. The War Office also requisitioned land at Dalmilling, Dam Park and at Fulshawwood in order to create camps where various army divisions were stationed in huts.

Iron and other metals were collected for the war effort, and many fine railings in the town disappeared in April 1942. One of the saddest losses was the railing that surrounded Burns' Statue in its Square. These had incorporated ornate posts decorated with lions and thistles, topped with lamps. Something else that disappeared at this time was the tank that had sat on the Low Green since the First World War.

Air-raid shelters and first aid posts were established in different areas to deal with the casualties of any attacks that reached the county. The nearest first aid post to Ayr was established in Allan's Garage, in Prestwick's Main Street, which had four casualty-carrying vans. Shelters and Nissen huts were established in various locations throughout the town and in November 1940 an additional sixteen were erected. The historic John Welch Garden off the High Street was covered in shelters, much to the disgust of the Reverend Archibald MacKenzie, who wrote a short history of it in *Ayrshire Collections*, describing it as 'one of the most sacred and historic places in Ayr'. (John Welch was a minister of the church in Ayr from 1600 until 1605; he married a daughter of John Knox and is said to have saved Ayr from the plague.)

Ayr Town Council established an Air Raid Patrol, but it insisted that it was to be on a purely part-time and voluntary basis, being concerned at the possible cost. The ARP appointed wardens to check for lights showing at night. The ARP Ambulance Service was set up and Ayr had eight ambulances, six of which had been converted from private cars. A Cadet Corps of school-aged pupils had been in existence from before the Great War. With the outbreak of war once more it recruited record numbers. It was eventually disbanded in 1949. Also in existence was the Air Training Corps, which met in the Academy.

When Italy joined the war in June 1940, supporting Germany, there was a backlash against Italians living in the town. A number of disturbances were recorded, including the ransacking of a shop at Lochside and the burning of a kiosk on the Low Green, both of which were operated by Italians. The police arrested forty Italian residents, both for their own safety and to vet them for national security purposes.

Ayr harbour was busier than ever during the war period. It became home to a number of minesweepers as well as naval escort vessels. The shipyard, which had been scheduled for closure in 1939, was taken over for the war effort and used for maintenance work. When the Admiralty proposed returning the yard to its owners in August 1943 the workers campaigned against it. At Spring Gardens, beyond Greenan, a Royal Navy camp was established in 1942, known as HMS Scotia, where four thousand ratings were trained in signals, communications and other skills. Ayr Barracks, which had been in existence since 1794, were renamed the Churchill Barracks in 1942 after Sir Winston Churchill, who had commanded the 6th Battalion Royal Scots Fusiliers, based at Ayr Barracks, during the Great War.

A new aerodrome was constructed at Heathfield and opened in April 1941. This was initially home to the Spitfires of the 602 (City of Glasgow) Squadron of the Royal Air Force, which had just returned from front-line service in the Battle of Britain. In the summer of that year, the Hurricanes of 43 Squadron and the Beaufighter and Defiant night-fighters of 141 Squadron joined them. In the year that Heathfield aerodrome was opened, a Liberator aeroplane, operated by the Atlantic Ferry Organisation and bound for Canada, crashed during take-off. On striking the ground the fuel tanks caught fire, burning the fuselage with such a heat that no rescue attempt was possible. The twenty-two air force personnel were all killed in the inferno, and were laid to rest in Holmston cemetery. At a later date eleven of the dead (who were American civilian ferry pilots and navigators) were disinterred and moved to a Cambridge cemetery. The folk of the district subscribed to a memorial that was laid in the grass at Holmston:

A
TOKEN OF RESPECT
TO 22 VICTIMS OF AIR CRASH
AT WHITLETTS 14TH AUGUST 1941.
SUBSCRIBED FOR BY INHABITANTS OF WHITLETTS.
'FOR FREEDOM'

One of the dead was Arthur B. Purvis, chairman of the British Purchasing Commission. He had almost single-handedly persuaded the American government to sell vital war munitions and other supplies to Britain, and to withdraw such sales to Germany. His death was a disaster for the war effort, and Churchill referred to it in his memoirs.

Those who were not serving abroad risked little chance of injury during the war, though a few stray bombs did land in the area. A mine suspended on its parachute over Ayr harbour exploded at twenty past eleven on the night of 26 October 1940. A more serious incident was the arrival of a Heinkel bomber at ten o'clock on the night of 13 March 1941. A Blenheim aircraft of the 600 (City of London) Squadron intercepted the intruder. The Ground-Controlled Interception radar station that had been established at St Quivox earlier in the year initially guided the Blenheim towards its target, and when it was within a thousand yards of the Heinkel its own radar took over. Two attacks were made and the Heinkel crashed at Drumshang farm, one mile south of Dunure, half an hour later. The four crew in the Heinkel survived, though three of them suffered injuries. The Heinkel had been part of the bombing raid that made such a devastating impact on Clydeside, in particular at Clydebank and Greenock.

A team of Local Defence Volunteers was established in May 1940 to deal with any local emergency and provide the first line of defence in case of attack from Germany. The name was later changed to the Home Guard, but because of the age of most members it soon gained the nickname 'Dad's Army'. The Ayr Guard (7th Ayrshire Battalion) organised a number of roadblocks, manned air-raid shelters, and took part in camps at Croy Bay and

Dunure. The Home Guard played a vital part in maintaining order in the town, but was eventually given the orders to 'stand down' in 1944. In Ayr a Stand Down Parade was held in November that year, followed by a ceremony on Sunday 3 December.

Prisoners of war were billeted all over the county, one of the local camps being established at Doonfoot, where Italian prisoners were held. An attempted escape occurred in December 1944 and as late as 1948 one inmate died following a hunger strike there.

The local hospitals were included in the government's Emergency Hospital Scheme, which designated beds for the sole purpose of treating casualties of air raids and other military activity. Ayr County Hospital at first had forty such beds, but when it was realised that the number of casualties requiring treatment was not as bad as expected, twenty of these were returned to general use. The hospital treated a number of casualties, the greatest number being in 1944, when the south-east of England was subject to regular flying-bomb attacks. In that year twenty-eight patients from Hillend Hospital in St Albans were evacuated to the County Hospital.

The bombing of the south-east of England also resulted in a few relocations. Early in 1941 the London Metallic Capsule Co. moved to Ayr after its own factory had been destroyed in the blitz. The firm, which made screw caps for bottles, acquired what had been Beavan's Garage in Burns' Statue Square and resumed manufacture. So good were the local workers that production increased by one third, and the firm made plans to establish a purpose-built factory in the burgh.

Not everyone did their best for king and country. There were many that saw the war as an opportunity to make a dishonest penny. There was also the case of James Simpson, a soldier from Fulham, London, who used his posting to Ayr to make a bigamous marriage Emily Lauder, while he still had a wife living at Gravesend in Kent.

The war ended in 1945 with the declaration of peace. The town was glad to return to peaceful times, though the effects of war still existed. Many foodstuffs were still rationed, and remained so for a number of years. At the cenotaph new panels were added to the Great War memorial, listing the 263 men who had paid the ultimate sacrifice for their country. Other memorials were erected in schools (Ayr Academy's memorial lists seventy-eight former pupils), factories and churches. The Auld Kirk had a new oak pulpit constructed as a war memorial, copying the style of the original pulpit that had been removed in 1882.

A war graves plot was laid out in Holmston cemetery, and numerous army, navy and aircraft personnel were laid to rest there. The standard military headstone was erected over their graves, inscribed with little more than name, rank, number, date of death and their regimental badge.

After the war the Council tried to catch up with the demand for housing. Building work, which had been halted in 1939, was completed, and proposals for thousands of new council houses were made, in response to a demand for three thousand new homes. The housing shortage was so severe that 160 prefabs were erected as a temporary measure. More permanent Swedish-style houses were erected at Mainholm, the first of them, at 1 Westwood Avenue, being officially opened on 1 December 1946 by Rt. Hon. Joseph Westwood MP, Secretary of State for Scotland. Those who could still not get a home squatted in the former army camps, some remaining for a good number of years.

The hero of the war, Sir Winston Churchill, came to Ayr to attend the annual conference of the Scottish Unionist Association in May 1947. He was granted the Freedom of the Burgh, the Council having voted by ten to eight (the Labour members unanimously voted against) to offer this honour.

22

DOON THE WATTER

AYR HAS BEEN A leading holiday resort for more than a century. The coastal location, and the miles of golden sands affording fine views of the mountains of Arran, has been used to sell the town to generations of visitors. Holidays at Ayr began in earnest in the nineteenth century when the railway arrived, and the town became the ideal place for Glaswegians to head for a breath of fresh sea air. The wealthy were the first to arrive: many Glasgow merchants built holiday homes for themselves all along the Clyde Coast, and Ayr was an integral part of this process. For example, Glendoon House (now the Fairfield House Hotel) was built for a Glasgow tea merchant.

A few new inns and hotels were developed in the early nine-teenth century, among them the Burns Arms Inn at Alloway in 1829 (now the Brig o' Doon Hotel). Many of the larger houses in the town were converted into hotel establishments, including the Hotel Dalblair, Sea Tower and Redhouse (renamed Savoy Park). Milrig House in Charlotte Street (demolished 1970) was converted into a hotel in 1860. It had a large garden that boasted a tennis court, putting green, summerhouse and swings. On offer were luncheons and teas, and the hotel advertised itself as a 'cyclists' rest'. The largest hotel in the town for many years was the Station Hotel, which opened for business in 1886.

Some of the hotel advertisements from the period make inter-esting reading. The Sea Tower Private Hotel promoted itself thus:

Situated in own grounds. Well-kept flower and herbaceous garden. Croquet, etc. Adjacent to Belleisle Golf Course. Beach three minutes from gate. Buses pass gates for Town, Station (three minutes), and Burns Country. Hot and Cold, and Gas Fires in all

Bedrooms. Interior springs in all Beds. Home Baking. Chef
Cuisine. Central Heating. Honeymoon Hotel gives you just the
RIGHT start in life.

There were also many small private hotels and guesthouses,
many of them long forgotten. From a long list, it is worth men-
tioning the Arrandale, Bonnie Doon, Castleview, Darlington,
Ellands, Firknowe, Glencanisp, Green Gables, The Rise, St
Catherines, and Woodcroft.

Throughout the nineteenth century steamers plied from
Glasgow 'doon the watter' to piers at a variety of coastal resorts.
One of the stopping points was Ayr, where a couple of hours could
be spent before sailing back up the Clyde. The *Vale of Clyde* was
one of the steamers offering sails at this time. It left the city at
seven o'clock in the morning, reached Ayr in time for lunch at
half-past twelve, set sail once more at half-past two and arrived
back in the city, with a tired but happy group of passengers, at
eight o'clock in the evening.

Excursions on steamers were also available from Ayr. The
Countess of Glasgow, which was mastered by John MacArthur, sailed
from the town to various ports on the Firth of Clyde. Destinations
included Arran, Campbeltown, Stranraer, Arrochar, Kyles of Bute and
even Belfast. Sails were advertised in local newspapers:

> Pleasure Trip to Roseneath
> The *Countess of Glasgow* will sail from Air for Roseneath
> on Thursday the 23rd June curt.
> At Five o'clock morning,
> calling at Troon, Ardrossan and Largs, in going and returning.
> Fares, cabin 5s. steerage 3s.
> Air, 16th June 1831.

One of the Council's first attempts at making the beach more
attractive for visitors was to build the Esplanade. This extends
south from the harbour towards Doonfoot, a distance of two
miles. The first stretch of it was constructed in 1881 and further
extensions were completed in 1925. However, plans mooted in
1899 for a pier with a bandstand at its end – in the style of many
English resorts – did not come to fruition.

The beach was Ayr's principal attraction. In the Edwardian years it was lined with bathing machines that allowed women to change into their bathing costumes. The machines were then hauled across the sands to the water by horse, allowing the bathers to slip into the water. It was the Council's Attraction Committee that introduced these machines in 1902.

A number of guides to the town and its attractions for holidaymakers were published over the years. The *Penny Guide to Ayr and Alloway* was published by the Ayr Publishing Company in 1885, listing the town's many attractions and detailing the history of places of interest. By the twentieth century the town was promoted as *Ayr for Health, Rest and Recreation* (published by the Ayr Attractions Committee) and later as *Ayr for Health and Pleasure*. The *Penny Guide* contained verses that were designed to attract holidaymakers:

I looked me from my casement forth,
Upon a scene surpassing fair,
Outvieing all on Tay or Forth,
It was the glorious Bay of Ayr.

In 1870 an anonymous writer compiled *Ayr as a Summer Residence*, in which he detailed some of the attractions of the burgh. These included the fact that the town had no large factories polluting the 'full supply of pure, vital air', it had a safe beach where 'deaths from drowning very seldom occur', bands and troupes of performers entertained, and there were sports for men and women alike. The guide also notes that:

The Auld Toon o' Ayr is year by year increasing in favour as a Summer resort, more especially with the Glasgow folks, the Railway communication being so convenient for business men who require to visit the city every morning. From the beginning of May to the end of September, there is a constant demand for houses, but more especially in July and August and the race week in September. . . . As might naturally be expected from its situation, Ayr is an exceedingly healthy place, having always a cool refreshing breeze from the sea, and in general a pure, invigorating, and exhilarating atmosphere. . . . The best proof which can be given of the popularity of Ayr as a summer resort is that, year after year, many who have only come to spend the summer months settle down as permanent residents.

Ayr's famous beach and esplanade

Attractions for holidaymakers were created at various times along the Low Green and Esplanade. A boating pond had paddle-boats and rowing boats for hire, and putting greens were located near Wellington Square. The 'shows' or funfair regularly appeared on the Esplanade, run by the Codona family. In June 1934 the *Pageant of Ayrshire* celebrated the county's history and culture with a large festival held at the Dam Park.

The Glasgow Fair was one of Ayr's busiest times. The city folk were keen to leave the overcrowded suburbs and head for the fresh air and bracing breezes at the coast. In the 1950s fourteen additional trains were laid on between Glasgow and Ayr, and Western Omnibuses put on ninety extra buses to cope with the passengers and their luggage. It has been estimated that in 1955 20,000 visitors came to the town on one day. Tales of the Glasgow visitors are legion, such as buying deckchairs at Woolworths, using them for the day, then returning them to the shop on some pretext or another and getting a full refund. Many houses in the town let out rooms on a self-catering basis to families of the lower classes. These families often returned year after year to the same residence.

Paddle-steamers plied their trade from the harbour and for many Victorian and Edwardian visitors a sail was an essential part of the holiday experience. The *Bonnie Doon* was operated from 1876 until 1880 by Seath and Steele from Glasgow's Broomielaw to Ayr. A first-class ticket cost three shillings and sixpence. From the burgh it took passengers on excursions to Campbeltown and Arran. The vessel had a number of mechanical faults, earning it the sobriquet 'Bonnie Breakdoon'. The *Waverley* (the first vessel to bear the name) sailed from Ayr between 1885 and 1887.

The celebrated passenger steamer, the *Juno*

The Glasgow and South Western Railway Company was granted the right to operate steamers in 1892, and from 1898 until 1931 operated the *Juno*. Built by Barclay, Curle and Company at Clydebank, the *Juno* sailed from Ayr to Arran, and made a once-weekly trip to Stranraer. In 1932 the *Duchess of Hamilton*, which had been built in 1890 for the Caledonian Steam Packet Company, replaced this popular vessel. Other notable steamers plying from Ayr included the *Glen Sannox*, built in 1892 by J. and G. Thomson of Clydebank. At the time of her launch she proved to be the fastest ship on the Clyde, which turned out to be good for attracting trade.

The outbreak of war killed off these sailings for a time, but in 1947 cruises from the harbour recommenced. Steamer sails resumed in 1974, and continue to sail at the time of writing, when the last ocean-going paddle-steamer in the world, PS *Waverley*, makes Ayr one of its ports of call.

The former HMS Scotia camp at the Heads of Ayr was acquired by Billy Butlin in 1947 and converted into a holiday camp, complete with 'Sunshine Chalets', entertainment and fairground rides. The chair lift was salvaged from an old coal-mine, and proved to be a popular attraction. Holidays at Butlins were popular thereafter, 3,500 visitors coming every season. The camp was even referred to in song by Billy Connolly, but with the advent of the cheap package holiday to Spain and Greece, the traditional camp holiday declined. Even after upgrading to 'Wonderwest World' in 1988 the site was not as successful as it once was, and eventually was sold by the company to Haven Holidays who demolished the chalets, replaced them with static caravans, and renamed the park Craig Tara.

23
POPPLEWELL'S PLEASURE PALACES

THE POPPLEWELL FAMILY IS one that seems inextricably linked with Ayr, through its long association with the Gaiety Theatre and the Pavilion. The family came to Ayr from Yorkshire, initially expecting to remain for a few years, but found the town so congenial that they stayed for decades!

Leslie Benjamin Popplewell (or 'Young Ben' as he was known in his early days – he later became known as 'Daddy Ben') was born in Bradford on 13 March 1870. He was the second son of John Popplewell, an alderman in the town and proprietor of the family business of Popplewell Brothers, stockbrokers. John was also an honorary choirmaster, which helped to instil the love of performing in young Ben. In his youth he loved to build models of theatres from old wooden boxes, creating the scenery and actors from cuttings taken from the *Illustrated London News*. The actors were moved across the stage on the end of lengths of wire, and he charged friends either a halfpenny or a penny to watch performances.

Ben started off his working life as a stockbroker, employed in the family firm as a junior partner, but his love of the theatre began to grow. He became fascinated by the Saturday night concerts held in the town's Mechanics' Institute. Around 1887 Ben made his first appearance on a concert platform, and by his twentieth birthday he was in business for himself. He married Sarah (or Sally) Elizabeth Illingworth in 1895. Her father had also been an alderman in Bradford. They had four children, Charles Leslie (1898-1986), George Eric, Kathleen and Winifred.

In 1901, during the stock exchange's three-month closed period,

Ben sang and played the banjo with an act known as 'The Yorkshire Pierrots' at Clacton-on-Sea, somewhat to the surprise of his family. The leader of the Pierrots was Fred Pullan, and he and Ben became close friends. They were later to collaborate in directing and performing concerts at the Mechanics' Institute.

In 1904, when the Bradford Exhibition was dismantled, Ben purchased the temporary wooden concert hall. It had an elaborate frontage and was rebuilt at Frizinghall, where it was named the Al Fresco Theatre. It was opened in 1905 and 'The Dandy Militaires', comprising a local double act, 'The Musical Bentleys', with Ben Popplewell, were the first act to take the stage. One of the regular members of the audience was a youthful J.B. Priestley, who was later to use much of the knowledge he gained of the theatre in his book *The Good Companions*.

By 1907 Popplewell had bought a former coffee-house in Shipley, Yorkshire, which he converted into a variety theatre known as the Queen's Palace. The Bentleys had proposed moving the Al Fresco Theatre to a different site, resulting in the partnership splitting up. Ben operated the Queen's while attempting to carry on his work in stockbroking. He also held shares in a number of theatres across the country, one of these being the Council-owned Pavilion in Ayr. These shares fell in value in the time he held them, and, curious to find out why, he paid a visit to Ayr where he discovered that the Council had no idea how to run a theatre. After a long discussion he was invited to take over the running of the Pavilion as manager. He sold the Shipley theatre which was then converted into a cinema.

On 2 May 1913 Ben Popplewell leased the Pavilion on the Low Green, retaining it for five years. Proposals for a Pavilion had been mooted as early as 1903 when ex-Bailie Wallace Allan had suggested it. The building was opened by Provost James S. Hunter on 23 May 1911 as part of a scheme to attract visitors to the town. The building cost £8,000 to build and contained 1,500 seats with room for a further 1,000 to stand. The design, which was rather eclectic, was the work of local architect J.K. Hunter, who won an open competition. The building was soon to be derided as the 'White Elephant by the Sea'.

On acquiring the lease to the Pavilion, Ben Popplewell moved to Ayr, living at 4 Barns Terrace. Ben was keen to attract as many big names as possible to the town, and within weeks the Lancastrian ukulele player, George Formby, appeared. W.F. Frame also starred for a week in June.

In 1918 Ben Popplewell bought himself a racehorse. Star o' Doon was noted for having won at Ayr racecourse on more than one occasion, but by this time he was ready for retiring. Popplewell used the horse for promotional purposes for a time, before selling it on. The money raised was used to endow a bed at Seafield Hospital. Generosity was one of Popplewell's great attributes.

With the end of the Pavilion lease in November 1918 Ben Popplewell returned south, where he purchased the Coliseum Theatre in Goole, Yorkshire, as well as a picture house near Leicester. Leslie and Eric were in charge of the cinema side of the business, for Ben had lost interest in the cinema with the arrival of the 'talkies', and instead spent more time developing his interests in the theatre. The call of Ayr was still strong, and when the Pavilion lease came up again he jumped at the chance. The decision to return was also influenced by the illness of Kathleen (Pattie) Popplewell. The industrial atmosphere of Bradford was not helpful, and the fresh sea breezes of Ayr were thought to be ideal for aiding recovery. Unfortunately, however, she died in 1923.

The Popplewell family took over the Pavilion once more on 1 May 1922 and continued to offer entertainment there until giving up the lease in 1967. The Pavilion was used for a variety of purposes over its lifetime under Popplewell management. It presented top-class variety shows that were popular with visitors. Charlie Kemble's Entertainers were brought in 1923, and ran from 1926 until 1930, playing to capacity audiences. This was followed by the Ayr Entertainers, which included the comedians Pete Martin and Charlie Holbein, as well as Colin Murray and Grace Clark, styled 'Mr and Mrs Glasgow', who were to settle in the town. The Merrymakers concert party was one of the biggest draws, having to increase the number of performances during the summer months to two per night. One of the Merrymakers' shows was broadcast on BBC radio in 1932. Other entertainment such as boxing matches, roller-skating, film shows and dancing have been held within its large hall. In 1934 Popplewell celebrated twenty-one years as lessee of the Pavilion and he noted that there was no other town of comparable size to Ayr where so many stars had played. At the outbreak of the Second World War the Pavilion was requisitioned for military use.

In 1925 Ben Popplewell purchased the Gaiety Theatre in Carrick Street. It had been built to the plans of Ayr architect, J. MacHardy Young, at a cost of £9,500. When it was opened, on 6 September 1902, it could accommodate an audience of 1,200, facing a stage forty-seven feet wide by thirty feet deep. The first professional production to be presented was 'The Brixton Burglary', which was staged on Monday 8 September. The auditorium was packed to capacity, and disappointed folk had to be turned away. The Gaiety soon afterwards suffered a major fire, with the result that it had to be rebuilt. Alex Cullen supervised the restoration of the rococo interior and it was reopened in 1903. At this time the building was renamed the New Gaiety Theatre. In that year lectures on health were on offer, and other early attractions included the first movies imported from America.

After the Gaiety came into Popplewell ownership, it was operated by a partnership formed of Ben and his two sons, although Leslie was mainly responsible for overseeing the Pavilion. After two seasons the family realised that Ayr could hardly support two major theatres, so they decided to convert the Pavilion into a ballroom, leaving the more suitable Gaiety building as the home of variety and music hall artists. The Pavilion still had numerous international stars playing in it, including Kenny Ball's Jazzmen, Acker Bilk, George Melly and Humphrey Lyttleton.

After acquiring the Gaiety, Ben Popplewell continued to introduce many top-class acts to the town. At that time tickets for the shows ranged from three shillings and sixpence for a box seat down to sixpence for a gallery seat. Among the many stars who appeared in the early days were Ella Shields, Florrie Forde, Sid Field, Flanagan and Allen, George H. Elliott (advertised as 'The

Chocolate Coloured Coon'), Talbot O'Farrell, Bransby Williams, Albert Whelan, Reg Maxfield, and the Scottish magician, Dr Walford Bodie. It was Ben Popplewell who brought Flanagan and Allen together. In 1923 Florrie Forde telephoned Ben to see if he could recommend a partner for Chesney Allen, his original partner having left at short notice. Ben thought of Bud Winthrop, who was appearing solo as a comedian in Kilmarnock's Palace Theatre. The pair clicked instantly, Winthrop adopting the stage name Flanagan from a song Florrie Forde sang in the show. Later in life, when asked what famous acts had appeared at the Gaiety, Ben would smile and reply that it would be easier for him to list the famous acts that had not appeared!

To ensure a packed auditorium, Popplewell arranged for buses to transport audiences from their homes as far afield as Maybole and Cumnock. Big acts like Jose Collins, Wee Georgie Wood, and Layton and Johnstone ensured the customer wanted to come, and such was Popplewell's reputation in the business that many performers were willing to appear for a fraction of what they could earn elsewhere.

The celebrated Scots comedian Will Fyffe was a Popplewell discovery. His father ran a penny geggie, or portable theatre, in which he gained a grounding in performing. After his appearance at the Pavilion as an unknown comic in 1914, earning a half share of £8, Ben Popplewell encouraged him, and he made his Gaiety debut in September 1926. At first he used material which Harry Lauder had discarded, but he became famous for his own monologues and songs, of which 'I belong tae Glasgow' must be his best known. Fyffe married Lily Bolton, daughter of a partner in Pearson and Bolton, owners of the old geggie that stood in Carrick Street. A wooden structure, it had the grand title of 'Caledonian Theatre'.

Other stars that Popplewell encouraged and set off on the road to stardom were the comedian Lex McLean, Dave Willis and Jack Anthony. Many were regulars in the Gaiety Whirl. The Whirl had its origins as a summer show in 1930, which was a resounding success. In the following summer it appeared again, with the title 'Whirl of Gaiety'. Again a major attraction, the summer shows were repeated thereafter, from 1932 being known as the Gaiety Whirl. The Whirl of 1935 saw the debut of Denny Willis. In 1938 Mervyn Saunders was part of the Whirl. During the season he was married to Barbara Hislop and the reception was held on the Gaiety's stage, which was laid out to look like the dining room of a luxury cruise liner. Other acts in that season's Whirl were involved: Scots comedian Jack Anthony was the best man and 'My Brother and I' (Alf and Bob Pearson) were the ushers.

For one week only from Monday 2 October 1933 the famous Scots comedian and singer, Harry Lauder, appeared on the Gaiety stage, his only appearance as a solo act. Lauder had previously been in Ayr with a concert party, but at that time he was an unknown, and, in addition to his comedy act, had to carry the piano and post bills around the town. He also appeared in a few of G.L.W. Connell's Saturday evening concerts, and prior to this his last performance in Ayr had been in 1904 when he was part of a concert party which performed there en route to Ireland. Lauder's week on the Gaiety stage was so popular that the charge for orchestra stall seats was raised fifty per cent to three shillings. He played a large part in the variety show, performing 'It's a' roon the toon' and 'Waggle o' the kilt' in the first half; 'When I was twenty-one' and 'Flower o' the heather' in the second. His best number in the show was 'Boss o' the hoose' in which he acted the part of a poor country joiner who used to be kept under his wife's domineering thumb – but he liked her well enough now that she was dead!

In 1938 the façade of the Gaiety was rebuilt in a style typical of the time. A couple of years later Ben Popplewell reached the age of seventy and decided to retire. The business was kept going under the management of his sons, Eric and Leslie, and his daughter, Winnie. Sitting in the 1942 Gaiety Whirl audience was the Duke of Kent, who greatly enjoyed the show. Unfortunately he was to suffer injuries in a plane crash in the Highlands a few days later.

More recent acts that honed their craft at the Gaiety include Margo Henderson (first appearing at the age of fourteen), local lass Moira Anderson, Kenneth McKellar and Johnny Beattie. Johnny Beattie made his first appearance in 'Cinderella' in 1953.

Popplewell's Gaiety Theatre

All went on to become recognised names in the world of Scottish entertainment.

Ben Popplewell died on Tuesday 7 February 1950 at his home at 17 Bellevale Avenue. His wife had died ten years before. His funeral at Holmston cemetery was attended by hundreds of mourners, including a number of well-known actors. Close friends, Jack Anthony and Dave Willis were there, the latter stating, 'The profession has today lost one of its best friends. There are few like him left in it.' Tributes were paid from friends all over Britain, including some from London theatrical agents, some of the 1927 Gaiety Girls and members of the Gaiety Good Companions Club, which Popplewell had formed a number of years before. At the last night of the season's pantomime, producer Jack Barton paid tribute to Popplewell from the stage, noting with pride that the pantomime just finished had broken Gaiety records in playing to almost 100,000 people within eight weeks. Ben's estate was valued at £7,981 6s 5d.

The Popplewells also took over the Palace Cinema in Burns' Statue Square. They converted this into the Palais de Danse, which was a popular venue for ballroom dancing between the wars. This was later converted into the Bobby Jones Ballroom.

The Gaiety celebrated its golden anniversary in 1952. As part of the celebrations a radio programme entitled 'The Gaiety, Ayr' was broadcast on BBC radio. It was during this period, from 1950 to 1953, that Jimmy Logan and the Logan Family entertained on stage. Calum Kennedy first appeared at the Gaiety in October 1963.

Another of the Gaiety 'discoveries' was Andy Stewart, who first appeared in 1955 as a front-cloth comic to Clark and Murray (Mr and Mrs Glasgow). He was later to hit the pop charts with his rendition of 'Scottish Soldier', and become synonymous with all things Scottish. Jack Milroy appeared in 1954 and returned for the following six seasons. He appeared on stage in some of those seasons with Glen Michael, another Ayr entertainer, who later found television fame. Milroy was to become renowned for his double act with Rikki Fulton called 'Francie and Josie'. The pair graced the stage in a sell-out concert in 1971-2.

The Gaiety was destroyed by fire again on 2 August 1955. Fire engines from Ayr and Kilmarnock attended the blaze, but the roof collapsed and much of the building was destroyed. A temporary roof had to be raised over the building to prevent the weather from destroying what remained. The Popplewell family decided to restore the building, which took some time to achieve. The restoration work, which cost £60,000, reduced the theatre's capacity to 572 seats. The Gaiety reopened on 2 July 1956 and the Popplewell brothers received a telegram from the Queen congratulating them on the restoration.

The Popplewells sold the Gaiety and the business on 22 March 1965 to Glasgow Pavilion Theatre, who bought the entire share capital of Ben Popplewell and Sons for £65,000. Eric and Leslie remained as managers, and continued to bring big acts to the theatre.

Eric Popplewell decided to retire in 1972, and there was little prospect of replacing him. The theatre was sold in November that year to a developer named Telegraph Properties (Scotland) who proposed demolishing the building and erecting a shop and office complex on the site. Redevelopment plans did not include the building, and it was not until the theatre was listed for its fine rococo plasterwork that these were abandoned. After some deliberation, Ayr Town Council decided to buy the building for £72,000 on 1 November 1973 and following some refurbishment opened the theatre to the public once more in 1974.

The theatre continues to attract audiences to its productions, which range from the ever-popular Christmas pantomime through all sorts of shows to the perennial 'Gaiety Whirl'. More recent entertainers to appear at the theatre include the Aberdeenshire comedians 'Scotland the What?', 'City Lights' (from a television programme), and 'The Singing Kettle' for children. It has also been the setting for concerts by popular entertainers such as comedienne Dorothy Paul, singer Joe Longthorne, impressionist Gary Wilmot and singer Elkie Brooks. In 1996 a new box-office and café extension was added on the south-west side of the building, making the theatre ready to continue to entertain the public 'in the style of the Popplewells' into its second century.

24

THE HONEST MEN – FOOTBALL IN AYR

THERE IS A LONG and proud footballing tradition in Ayr. This encompasses not only Ayr United Football Club, formed in 1910, but also the plethora of clubs active from the early 1870s. The town has witnessed many successes. Teams from Ayr have reached three Scottish Cup semi-finals and two League Cup semi-finals. In addition Ayr United has frequently been in the higher echelons of the Scottish leagues. With the advent of the millennium, a fresh chapter is about to be written as the club has ambitious plans to move to a new stadium in the Heathfield area of the town.

The story of organised football can be traced to the early 1870s: Ayr Academy and Ayr Thistle were both formed in 1872. By the mid-1870s other teams had been established, including Ayr Eglinton, Ayr Albert and Ayr Victoria. Most matches were played on the Low Green or at the Old Racecourse. However, Ayr Thistle proved the most enterprising and developed their own ground at Robbsland Park, off St Leonard's Road.

By season 1876/7 teams from Ayr were competing in the Scottish Cup, then in its fourth season. Indeed they were doing so to some effect. Ayr Thistle reached the semi-final in 1877 and were drawn to play against Vale of Leven. The pundits gave Thistle little chance: Vale of Leven had inflicted the first-ever defeat on the mighty Queen's Park in the previous round. The experts, sadly, were proved right as Ayr Thistle slumped to a 9–0 defeat at Kinning Park, then the home of Rangers FC. It would be a long wait before supporters could enjoy another such cup run; ninety-six years were to elapse before Ayr United reached the semi-final in 1973.

Despite this defeat, football continued to grow in popularity. The number of local teams clearly illustrates the trend: Ayr Bonnie Doon, Ayr Robert Burns and Ayr Invicta were among those formed in the Victorian period. However, the most significant event was the amalgamation, in 1879, of the town's two most powerful clubs, Ayr Thistle and Ayr Academicals into Ayr FC. The new club, which originally played at Springvale Park, attracted many leading teams to the town in the 1880s, including Queen's Park, Aston Villa and Rangers. The team was also a regular competitor in the Ayrshire Cup, which had been inaugurated in 1877, and contested many cup-ties with fierce local rivals, Kilmarnock.

By the late 1880s Ayr FC played at Beresford Park which, to the considerable chagrin of the club, was taken over for part of the year by the organisers of the Cattle Show. Thus, in 1888, Ayr FC made the historic move to the new stadium in Somerset Road and the first match played there was against Aston Villa. The team did not disappoint its loyal supporters and the English giants were beaten by three goals to nil. However, Ayr FC did not have the town to itself. A new club, Ayr Parkhouse, was formed in 1886 and in 1888 moved to Ayr FC's former ground at Beresford Park. In addition, Ayr Athletic was formed around this time and, by the early 1890s, the town, remarkably, had three senior clubs.

While Ayr clubs competed fiercely throughout the 1890s in knock-out competitions, such as the Scottish Cup, Scottish Qualifying Cup and Ayrshire Cup, the main priority was entry to the Scottish League which had been formed in 1890. Ayr FC achieved this distinction in 1897 and the club's first league fixture in the Second Division was against Linthouse at Somerset Park. Despite the historic significance, the home team lost 4–1 to their Glasgow rivals. By 1903 the town had two teams in the Scottish League when Ayr Parkhouse were also accepted into the Second Division.

However, despite the prestige which came with having two league clubs, many supporters on both sides could see the benefits of a merged club and, in particular, the prospect of reaching the First Division. Therefore, after a couple of abortive attempts, Ayr FC and Ayr Parkhouse amalgamated to form Ayr United in 1910.

This, in itself, was historic: it was the only occasion in the history of Scottish football when two Scottish League clubs from the same town have merged.

The new club, nicknamed the Honest Men and playing in crimson and gold strips, was an instant success. In season 1910/11, Ayr United were runners-up in the Second Division, and proceeded to top the division in both seasons 1911/12 and 1912/13. The club was deservedly promoted to the First Division of the Scottish League for season 1913/14. Despite the advent of the First World War in 1914, league football continued and Ayr United performed creditably among the elite. Indeed the club achieved its highest-ever position in the Scottish game when finishing in fourth place in season 1915/16, with only Celtic, Rangers and Morton above them.

There was no shortage of talent in the Ayr United ranks at this time. Jimmy Richardson, who had won an English championship medal with Sunderland, was signed from the Wearsiders in 1914. A dashing centre forward, he would later play for Scotland against England. Willie McStay, a left-back, was loaned by Celtic to Ayr in 1912 and became captain of the side. Neil McBain, one of the greatest figures in the club's history and also to become a Scotland international, was signed in 1914. He would later play for Manchester United, Everton and Liverpool. His managerial career included three spells with Ayr United and, unusually, a period as manager of Estudiantes in Argentina. He was also the oldest player ever to play in the English football league: as an emergency goalkeeper for New Brighton at the age of fifty-one years and four months.

The post-war period opened with Ayr United still in the First Division. Indeed, the club would retain top-flight status until 1924/5, and win promotion again to the First Division again in 1927/8. Many notable wins were achieved in those years. In 1922 the first win at Celtic Park was recorded, and by no less than four goals to one. There was a famous victory over Rangers in the Scottish Cup of 1923 when a record Somerset crowd of 15,853 witnessed a 2–0 triumph over a powerful team that would become Scottish champions. Perhaps the most satisfying result of all was the single-goal defeat of Kilmarnock in the Scottish Cup of 1924. A new record crowd for Somerset of 16,721 witnessed the encounter.

The club's exploits in the 1920s were, of course, due to the number of top-class players available. John Smith (nicknamed 'Fermer Jock', because his father owned a farm near Beith) and Phil McCloy, Ayr's two fullbacks, filled those positions for Scotland against England in the first-ever international at Wembley in 1924 (the game finished in a 1–1 draw). A number of other Ayr United players were honoured by Scotland in this decade, including Neil McBain, Johnny Crosbie and Jimmy Hogg.

However, there is one Ayr United player from this era who is remembered above all others. Jimmy Smith was signed from Rangers in 1927 and over the next two years his goal-scoring exploits were to earn him a place in the football hall of fame. During season 1927/8, when Ayr United won the Second Division championship, Smith scored sixty-six league goals in only thirty-eight games. The tally included eleven games in which he scored a hat trick or better. This astonishing haul was accumulated at the rate of 1.74 goals per game. Smith's exploits make him the top scorer of all time in terms of league goals scored in a single season and, as such, have earned him a place in the record books. Given that modern defences are infinitely better organised than their inter-war counterparts, it is a record which is unlikely ever to be beaten.

The years from 1930 until the outbreak of the Second World War were generally good ones for Ayr United. In the ten seasons from 1929/30 until 1938/9, the club was only out of the First Division on one occasion (1936/7) and even in that season was relatively successful as the Second Division title was won. In the Scottish Cup, a new crowd record was set at Somerset Park in 1934 when 23,651 saw Celtic win 3–2. Among many excellent players from that time were Scotland goalkeeper Robert Hepburn, Billy Brae, Charles 'Fally' Rodger and Terry McGibbons. There was also Hyam Dimmer, who lived up to his exotic name with performances full of panache and skill.

The return of football after the Second World War saw Ayr

placed in the B Division of the Scottish League for season 1945/6. This was considered an injustice as Ayr had finished above several of the teams accorded A Division status. It was not a vintage period for the club; indeed, it would be the mid-1950s before the club returned to the top flight. Despite this Ayr played before some impressive crowds as football grew in popularity during the post-war years. In 1949, 20,584 gathered at Somerset to see Morton beat Ayr 2–0 in the Scottish Cup, while a year later 23,000 were at Rugby Park to watch the Ayrshire derby. In 1951, 22,152 gathered at Somerset to witness Ayr and Motherwell fight out a 2–2 draw in the Scottish Cup. In fact, the only real high point of these years came in cup competition when, in season 1950/51, Ayr had an excellent run in the League Cup. After winning a qualifying group which included Dunfermline, Dumbarton and Kilmarnock, Ayr defeated Dundee United home and away in the quarter final to earn a semi-final tie with Motherwell. Disappointingly, the tie, which was played at Ibrox, finished 4–3 in favour of the Steelmen.

Despite the distinctly moderate league form, the team had its usual crop of outstanding players: Malky Morrison, a bustling centre forward; the quaintly named Kinnaird Ouchterlonie, an inside right; Len Round, an outstanding goalkeeper; and Norrie McNeil, a defensive stalwart. However, one player stands out above all others in the 1950s: the great Peter Price. Following a career path that began in the Ayrshire Junior ranks, Price had moved on to non-league soccer in England when he signed for Ayr United in 1955. His impact over the next seven years was sensational, as he scored no less than 225 goals, becoming the club's record goal-scorer in the process, a distinction he still holds. This included a haul of forty-five strikes in season 1955/6, and an even more impressive tally of fifty-five in 1957/8. His exploits helped the club to the Second Division Championship in 1958/9.

Other outstanding players who emerged in the second half of the 1950s included Sam McMillan (perhaps surprisingly for an inside-forward, the club's second highest goal-scorer), Bobby Stevenson and Willie Paton. Under the shrewd guidance of manager Jacky Cox, the team achieved some excellent results. In season 1959/60 Ayr trounced Rangers 3–0 at Ibrox, and then completed the double over the Old Firm by beating Celtic 3–2 at Parkhead. In fact, Ayr's final league position for the season, eighth, was one place above that of Celtic.

Four Ayr United stalwarts: Scotland internationalist Phil McCloy; record goal-scorer Jimmy Smith; hero of the 1970s, centre back Rikki Fleming; Fleming's defensive partner, Alex 'Sanny' McAnespie

The first half of the 1960s was a less happy time for the club. Relegated at the end of season 1960/61, Ayr languished in the Second Division for the next five seasons. The decline was severe: at the end of 1963/4 Ayr could manage only fourteenth place in the Second Division, and attendances at Somerset were often numbered in the hundreds. Such was the depth of the crisis that one national newspaper reported, in November 1964, that the directors were considering winding up the club. The end of season 1964/5 found Ayr languishing in second-bottom place in the Second Division; the club, officially, was the second worst team in Scottish football.

It is perhaps understandable that near the end of such a dismal run the club's long-suffering supporters paid little attention to the signing of an ageing outside left from Third Lanark in the summer of 1964. The signing turned out to be momentous: the player's name was Ally MacLeod.

To many, perhaps most, Ayr United supporters Ally MacLeod is the single most important person in the club's history. Initially captain of the side, Ally progressed to player-coach and was appointed manager in May 1966. His influence cannot be overestimated; in his own way he was as important to Ayr as Jock Stein to Celtic, Bill Shankly to Liverpool or Matt Busby to Manchester United.

In his first long spell at the club from 1964 to 1975 many of Ayr's most notable players emerged. Men such as John 'Spud'

Murphy, a hard-tackling left back. Dick Malone, a superb over-lapping right back, who went on to win an FA Cup winner's medal with Sunderland in 1973. Alex 'Dixie' Ingram, a fearless centre forward. Rikki Fleming, a classy centre back signed from Rangers, and his defensive partner Alex 'Sanny' McAnespie. Quintin 'Cutty' Young, a brilliant outside right who would later star for Coventry City and Rangers. Johnny Doyle, also a right-winger, later transferred to Celtic for a fee of £90,000. Johnny Graham, a wily midfielder bought from Hibs. Stan 'the Mighty' Quinn, a redoubtable centre half. Ally also signed a centre forward from Dunfermline who was nearing the end of his career: that player, Alex Ferguson, would later become the greatest manager in British football history with St Mirren, Aberdeen and Manchester United.

In the league the club enjoyed an unbroken spell of nine seasons in the top flight, from 1969/70 to 1977/8: six in the First Division and three in the newly created Premier League. In fact, in 1972/3 Ayr missed qualifying for Europe by just three points when the team ended the season in sixth place. There were many notable triumphs by a team which, on its day, feared no one. In a First Division match in September 1969 a record crowd of 25,225 was shoehorned into Somerset to see Rangers being defeated 2–1, with the Ayr goals coming from Cutty Young and Jacky Ferguson.

The team was equally formidable in the cup competitions. In October 1969, an epic encounter saw Ayr draw 3–3 after extra time with Celtic in a League Cup semi-final at Hampden Park. In a tight replay Celtic, who would go on to reach the European Cup final that season, edged out the Honest Men 2–1. There was an even more famous cup encounter against the other half of the Old Firm. In April 1973, the largest crowd ever to watch Ayr United (51,158) gathered at Hampden for the Scottish Cup semi-final. The 15,000 fans who travelled from Ayr thought the team had got off to the perfect start when Dixie Ingram powerfully headed home a free kick from Davie Wells. However, their hopes were cruelly dashed when referee Bobby Davidson controversially chalked off the 'goal' for offside; a decision that still rankles with Ayr United fans today. Needless to say, Rangers went on to win the tie, by two goals to nil.

There was a major blow for the club in 1975: Ally MacLeod announced he was leaving to become manager of Aberdeen. It was the end of an era. Ally had become a legend at Somerset and was even voted Ayr's Citizen of the Year in 1973. Although Ayr retained Premier Division status until 1978, and Ally returned for a very brief term as manager in season 1978/9, things would never quite be the same again.

The 1980s were generally undistinguished despite the presence of a trio of players who would later go on to achieve great things in the game. Stevie Nicol was transferred to the all-conquering Liverpool team for £300,000, and became captain of that great club. Alan McInally was sold to Celtic for £120,000 in 1984 and would later star for Aston Villa and Bayern Munich, before becoming a television and radio pundit. The final member of the trio, Robert Connor, was sold to Dundee for £50,000 but would later make a considerable name for himself as a member of the formidable Aberdeen team of the eighties (he would return to play for Ayr in the twilight of his career).

The return of Ally MacLeod for a third spell as manager in 1985 led to the formation of a team that took the Second Division title in 1987/8 (there were, by this time, three leagues in Scottish football: the Premier, First and Second Divisions). The team had a number of talented players including Henry Templeton, John Sludden and Ian McAllister. However, the defining moment of the 1980s came off the pitch. In early 1988, the multi-millionaire steel magnate David Murray made an audacious bid to buy the club. Murray, a former pupil of Alloway Primary School, had been an avid Ayr United supporter in his youth, and his grandfather had also been a director. Despite his impressive credentials the existing directors believed his offer undervalued the club and, to the consternation of many supporters, shareholders overwhelmingly rejected it. Later that year David Murray bought a controlling stake in Rangers and the rest, as they say, is history.

In the wake of the bid from Murray, the club appeared to tread water and the 1990s was another decade of relative underachievement. A succession of inexperienced managers was appointed in George Burley, Simon Stainrod and Gordon Dalziel. At the end of season 1994/5, there was an ignominious relegation to Division Two of the league (in effect the third division, as Scottish football had undergone yet another reconstruction, this time to four leagues of ten).

The elevation of Dalziel from senior player to manager was, at least initially, a success. The team won the Second Division championship in season 1996/7 and, after narrowly retaining First Division status in 1997/8, finished in a creditable third position in 1998/9 playing much attractive football in the process. But perhaps the sweetest moments came in the Scottish Cup and in the League Cup. In three successive seasons, Ayr knocked local rivals Kilmarnock out of major cup competitions. The first triumph was at Rugby Park in the 1996/7 League Cup. A crowd of 8,543 saw Robert Connor score the only goal of the game to send Premier League Kilmarnock tumbling out of the competition. It was Ayr's first win at Rugby Park for eight years and, given that the team was two leagues below Kilmarnock in the Second Division, it was a highly creditable result.

This was followed by two quite sensational victories over Killie in the Scottish Cup within the space of eleven months. In February 1998 Ayr and Kilmarnock were paired together in the fourth round of the competition. On the day of the match, Somerset Park was a quagmire and referee Hugh Dallas almost had to postpone the tie. Fortunately for Ayr, the game survived the elements and the team recorded a hard-fought victory by two goals to nil. The scorers for Ayr were Jim Dick and Ian Ferguson. But the best was yet to come. In January 1999 the two Ayrshire teams were again drawn together in the Scottish Cup and, as before, the Honest Men had home advantage. In a sensational match, First Division Ayr swept aside their Premier League opponents 3–0. The Ayr counters came from Andy Lyons and Andy Walker, who converted two penalties. The victory was made even more enjoyable for the home support when Ray Montgomerie, the Kilmarnock skipper, was ordered off.

There was also another Scottish Cup semi-final to savour. In season 1999/2000, following wins over Premier League sides Motherwell and Dundee, Ayr comfortably beat Partick Thistle 2–0 at Somerset in the quarter-final to move into the last four. The other qualifiers were Hibs, Aberdeen and Rangers. While most Ayr fans believed the team had a realistic chance of beating either Hibs or Aberdeen, few gave them much chance against Rangers. Unluckily for Ayr, they were paired against the Ibrox giants when the draw was made. The gap between the two clubs had become a chasm since their last semi-final encounter in 1973. In fact, one national newspaper calculated that the Rangers team had cost no less than £31 million to assemble, while the outlay for the Ayr team was around £310,000, or one per cent of the Rangers total! On a more positive note, the Ayr players always seemed to lift themselves for cup matches, and so around ten thousand Ayr fans travelled with genuine optimism to Glasgow for the game. However, they were to be sorely disappointed as the normally reliable strike-force of Gary Teale, Glynn Hurst and Neil Tarrant missed early chances. Rangers, packed with international stars such as Arthur Numan, Andrei Kanchelsis, Stefan Klos and Barry Ferguson, ran out easy winners, by seven goals to nil.

Nevertheless, the future for Ayr United looks healthy. Under a wealthy and progressive chairman, Bill Barr, the club is hoping to develop a new stadium in the north of the town at Heathfield, which will cost in excess of £6 million. While achieving planning permission is proving difficult because the proposed development incorporates retail outlets, the whole process has shown the depth of feeling for the club. At a special meeting of the Planning Committee of South Ayrshire Council in June 1999 more than eight hundred people packed the Citadel centre to hear passionate speeches in favour of the proposed development from, among others, Phil Gallie, Member of the Scottish Parliament, and John Dalton, a leading figure in the United for Heathfield organisation. In Ayr town centre, in the space of only a few hours, United for Heathfield also collected eight thousand signatures on a petition advocating a move to the new site. Although the Planning Committee agreed the plans for the new stadium, the application was called in by the Scottish Executive in Edinburgh and, at the time of writing (May 2000), it was the subject of an official enquiry set up by that body.

The club was also making plans significantly to strengthen the playing staff in the summer of 2000. The prize, of course, was promotion to the Scottish Premier League, expanded to twelve teams from season 2000/1. For most supporters of the Honest Men that day cannot come quickly enough.

25

FATHER OF THE COMMONS – SIR THOMAS MOORE

ONE OF THE LONGEST-SERVING and most eminent Members of Parliament to represent Ayr was Thomas Moore, known respectfully as 'The Colonel'. He served the town for almost forty years and was for a time 'Father of the Commons'.

Thomas Cecil Russell Moore was born on 16 September 1886, the younger son of upper-middle-class parents. His father was John Watt Moore, of Fintona in County Tyrone, and his mother was Mary Kirkpatrick, daughter of Alexander Kirkpatrick of Closeburn Castle in Dumfriesshire. The young Moore was educated at Portora Royal School followed by Trinity College, Dublin.

Thomas Moore joined the regular army in 1908. He served in France at the beginning of the Great War, but from 1916 to 1918 served in Ireland as a member of General Headquarters staff. At the end of the war he served in Russia for two years, before returning to Ireland for a further three years. He was twice mentioned in dispatches.

A colourful character, Moore was honoured with many decorations. He was made a Brevet Major, and given the OBE in 1918 and the CBE in 1920. A number of foreign countries also decorated him, including Serbia, which gave him the Order of the White Eagle. He received the Order of Merit in Hungary, and the Orders of St Anne and St Vladimir in Russia. He retired from the army in 1925.

His first marriage took place on 19 February 1925, to Jean Gemmill, widow of John Pettigrew of Glasgow. They had no children and she died on 6 February 1945. A memorial service was held for her in the Auld Kirk. Moore was married a second time, on 26 February 1950, to the widow of Robert Angus of Ladykirk, Penelope Sheppard. After Moore's death she lived on for a number of years at the family home of Bogside House, near Monkton.

Moore was an adherent of the Conservative and Unionist Party, and a member of the Conservative Club in Glasgow. In 1924 he stood for the Coatbridge division of Lanarkshire but was defeated. He stood as a Unionist candidate for Ayr Burghs in the by-election held in 1925, winning the seat over Patrick J. Dollan (later to become Lord Provost of Glasgow) with a majority of 2,788. The by-election was caused by the appointment of the previous MP, Sir John L. Baird, as Governor-General of Australia.

At all eight subsequent elections he was successful in retaining the seat, even after the parliamentary boundaries were redrawn in 1950, creating the Ayr Division of Ayrshire and Bute. His largest majority was 18,000, which he won at the election of 1931. The election of 1935 saw Moore, with 25,893 votes, beating the Labour candidate, Arthur Brady, who had only 13,274 supporters. At the July 1945 election he narrowly beat William Ross by 725 votes, Ross later being elected as MP for Kilmarnock, serving as Secretary of State for Scotland, and being created Lord Ross of Marnock. This was Moore's lowest-ever majority, the result no doubt reflecting the landslide victory won by the Labour Party at this election.

In terms of his place on the political spectrum, he was on the right of the Tory party. As Murray Tosh points out in his history of the Conservatives in Ayr, Moore was a staunch supporter of South Africa's membership of the Commonwealth in the 1950s, and an advocate of both capital and corporal punishment. He was also described as a friend of Hitler by one newspaper, following less than critical remarks he made about the Nazi regime in 1934 (this charge was, of course, strongly denied by Moore). In addition he supported appeasement, a stance adopted by most Tory MPs of the time, as well as very many British people.

He was an assiduous Parliamentarian, sponsoring no fewer than nine Acts of Parliament, which included the Slaughter of

Animals Act, and the Architects' Registration Act. During his time in London he lived in Albemarle Street, SW1, later moving to Regent's Park. He was knighted in the Coronation Honours of 1937. Following his knighthood, the councillors of Irvine granted him the Freedom of the Burgh. During the Second World War, Moore was appointed chairman of the Home Guard Joint Parliamentary Committee and carried out this role for the duration of hostilities. His regular column in the *Ayrshire Post* was eagerly read during the war years. Among his many business interests, Moore was chairman of Eastwoods and its subsidiaries, and chairman of Sarakan Products. He was a director of the General Accident Assurance Corporation as well as of Angallen Investment Co.

Moore was no stranger to controversy. In 1944 he and Alexander Sloan, MP for South Ayrshire, argued over the proposed Prestwick Airport, which lay in Sloan's constituency. Moore had pressed for Prestwick to be developed for many years. Sloan felt Moore was being wholly opportunistic on the issue of the airport. As far as Sloan was concerned, he was 'an Irishman who lived in London, and, by accident, represented a Scots constituency and was completely out of touch with the people in that particular area'.

Moore's interests were wide-ranging. He was a fellow of the Royal Geographical Society, and a trustee of the Royal Society for the Prevention of Cruelty to Animals, even though he was a keen huntsman. He acted as the RSPCA's Vice-President for a time and was a trustee of the International League for the Protection of Horses. He was also chairman of the Anglo-Italian Society for the Protection of Animals. In 1931 he became an honorary associate of the Royal Institute of British Architects. He loved books, and was a keen golfer, also being a member of the Golfers' Club of London. Other clubs he belonged to included St James's, the Carlton, and the Garrick in London, St Stephen's Green in Dublin, the Ulster Club in Belfast and the County Club in Ayr. Moore gifted a number of trophies to sporting clubs throughout Ayrshire. In 1932 he presented the Moore Trophy for golf. Others include the Moore trophies for football and for bowling.

After the war Moore was appointed a Freeman of the City of

London. He was also chairman of the Anglo-Hungarian Fellowship, and a Master of the Needlemakers Company.

On 20 September 1956, in the Queen's Birthday Honours, Sir Thomas Moore was created a Baronet, taking as his title Moore of Kyleburn. On his coat of arms his motto was 'I bend but will not break', and his arms reflected the herald's punning humour in that the shield displayed a chevron between two moorcocks, and for a crest he had a Moor's head between two daggers.

Moore was present at hundreds of public ceremonies in Ayr. He opened Troon swimming pool in 1932, the Odeon Picture House in 1935, the British Legion Hall in 1946, Ayr Community Centre in 1949 and the Fisherman's Institute foundations in 1961.

In May 1963, as longest-serving Member, Moore became the Father of the House of Commons. He retired from politics that year, having represented the town of Ayr for no less than thirty-nine years. On 30 October 1969 Moore was honoured by being given the Freedom of the Royal Burgh of Ayr. Provost Alexander S. Handyside bestowed the honour on Moore, who regarded this as one of the greatest honours he had ever been given.

One of his great interests was horse-racing. He owned several racehorses, and his stepson, Nigel Angus, trained most of them at Ayr's Cree Lodge stables. He was due to attend the opening of the flat racing season at Ayr on Monday 5 April 1971, but was taken ill; his four-year-old colt Dualin won the Cunningham Handicap Plate in his absence. Four days later, on Friday 9 April, he died, aged eighty-four. A memorial service was held in his honour in Ayr Auld Kirk. Since he had no sons, the baronetcy became extinct.

26

MISCARRIAGE OF JUSTICE –
THE ROSS MURDER AND
PADDY MEEHAN

AYR IS NOT A TOWN associated with crime, much less armed robbery and murder. It was therefore a great shock to its citizens
when, in July 1969, a bungalow in the affluent suburb of Seafield
was broken into and one of the elderly occupants murdered in
cold blood. However, this crime, heinous as it undoubtedly was,
would have unimaginable and unprecedented consequences for
the Scottish legal and political establishment. It also set in motion
a bloody train of events that led to more murder and mayhem on
the streets of Glasgow. The affair was undoubtedly one of the
most dramatic episodes in Scottish legal history.

Abraham Ross, aged sixty-seven, and his wife Rachel, aged
seventy-two, lived in Blackburn Place, just off one of Ayr's main
thoroughfares, Racecourse Road. They were wealthy business
people from a Jewish background, with interests in bingo halls.
On Saturday 6 July two men wearing hoods broke into their house
and attacked them. In the struggle which ensued, Mr Ross fought
courageously against one of the intruders and, when it seemed he
would get the upper hand on his assailant, the other thug beat him
savagely about the head with an iron bar. The robbers then used a
rope and nylon stockings to tie the Rosses' hands and feet together.
To force him to hand over the keys to his safe, the raiders merci-
lessly beat Mr Ross about the head and face. Having emptied the
safe of cash and valuables, and not wishing to alert police by making their getaway in the middle of the night, the robbers spent a
couple of hours drinking the couple's whisky before leaving the

house in the early hours of the morning. Mr Ross remembered hearing the two thugs address each other as Pat and Jim, and this was to become the crucial piece of evidence in the trial that followed.

Continuing their callous treatment of the couple, the robbers left the Rosses tied up on the floor, and they were not discovered until the Monday morning, fully thirty hours later, when the home-help arrived. They were weak and badly hurt, and both were rushed to Ayr County Hospital. The doctors treated them for serious bruising and slashes, but Rachel Ross's condition was so severe that she died on the Tuesday. The police now had a murder to investigate.

The reference to 'Pat and Jim' seemed familiar to the police and they immediately thought of Paddy Meehan and James Griffiths, two well-known Glasgow criminals. When it was discovered that they had been in the vicinity of Ayr on the night of the robbery, detectives set out to hunt them down. Meehan was arrested on 14 July and taken into custody at Ayr police station. He told the officers who arrested him, 'You are making the biggest mistake of your life. I can prove I was in Stranraer that night.' Nevertheless, he was remanded in Barlinnie Prison, charged with murder.

In a desperate attempt to provide himself with an alibi, Meehan gave police the name and address of his associate, James Griffiths. A group of detectives, with a warrant for the arrest of Griffiths, went to the flat at 14 Holyrood Crescent in Glasgow. The response from Griffiths was, to say the least, unexpected: the unsuspecting, and unarmed, officers were met with a hail of bullets. They had no option but to take cover as Griffiths fired indiscriminately at them and at passers-by. Armed with a shotgun and telescopic rifle, Griffiths wounded five police officers and two innocent civilians. He then managed to break out of the police cordon around his flat and drove at high speed to Possil Road, where he burst into the Round Toll Bar wearing two bandoliers of ammunition and still carrying his two weapons. He fired twice into the ceiling and then proceeded to shoot dead an innocent customer, William Hughes. Griffiths left the bar, still firing at anything that moved, and stole a lorry. He made his way to Kay Street, where he was cornered in a flat by armed police. Chief Superintendent Malcolm Finlayson and a colleague ran to the flat occupied by the gunman and, on looking through the letterbox, Finlayson saw Griffiths coming towards him. The detective tried to hit the gunman in the shoulder, but his aim was awry and the bullet struck Griffiths in the chest and killed him.

The actions of Griffiths convinced the authorities they were correct in charging Meehan with the crime. Indeed, to the complete dismay of the defence team, led by the formidable Glasgow criminal lawyer Joe Beltrami, the Crown issued a brief statement: 'With the death of Griffiths and the apprehension of Patrick Meehan, the police are no longer looking for any other person suspected of implication in the incident concerning Mr and Mrs Ross at Ayr.' In Scots law there is a presumption of innocence, and the statement by the authorities was hardly likely to help Meehan get the fair trial that was his entitlement.

Abraham Ross picked Meehan out at an identity parade at CID headquarters in Glasgow. Meehan was asked to repeat the words spoken by one of the intruders. Mr Ross, heavily sedated and probably still in shock, said immediately that Meehan was one of the men present in his house. In a surprising departure from accepted procedure, no other member of the identity parade was asked to speak.

The trial of Patrick Meehan took place in Edinburgh. His defence team took the view that if the jury was drawn from the citizens of Ayr and district he could not possibly get a fair trial. There may have been some truth in this argument: a crowd several hundred strong had gathered in Wellington Square to witness Meehan's initial appearance at Ayr Sheriff Court. Perhaps fired up by the extensive media coverage, the mob bayed for Meehan's blood. Despite the heavy police presence, the crowd lunged forward as Meehan was led into the court and he was kicked, punched and spat upon in the melee.

Meehan's defence team was thought to be the most formidable in Scotland at the time. Beltrami, the doyen of Glasgow criminal lawyers, was his instructing solicitor, while Nicholas Fairbairn QC was the senior counsel. Fairbairn, a colourful and flamboyant character later to become Member of Parliament for Perth and a minister in the government of Margaret Thatcher, was a brilliant advocate with an exceptional record in serious criminal cases. The team was completed by John Smith as junior counsel. Already a Member of Parliament, he would later become a Cabinet Minister and leader of the Labour Party.

With such an array of legal talent, Meehan had a fighting chance, and, given the paucity of the evidence against him, his acquittal seemed a strong probability. The case against him hinged on the dubious identification by Abraham Ross and flimsy circumstantial evidence. The most contentious piece of evidence centred on scraps of paper found in the pocket of a coat belonging to James Griffiths. The prosecution averred that they were identical to pieces of lining paper used in the Rosses' safe. Having 'established' that Griffiths and Meehan were accomplices, the prosecution went on to argue Meehan's guilt by association. The defence, of course, was highly sceptical: the suspicion was that the police had simply planted the scraps of paper to secure a conviction.

The defence attempted to counter the prosecution case in two ways. First, a plea of alibi was entered. Meehan freely admitted he and Griffiths had been in the vicinity of Ayr on the night in question. However, he claimed they were actually on their way to Stranraer to plan the theft of tax discs from the Motor Taxation Office, and several witnesses testified that they had seen Meehan and Griffiths in Stranraer on the fateful night. The second strand was the impeachment by the defence lawyers of another Glasgow criminal, Ian Waddell. It had been the talk of the Glasgow underworld for months that Waddell and an associate were responsible.

The trial lasted four days. It was a splendid battle of wits between a superb defence team and an equally formidable prosecution, led by the Solicitor-General for Scotland, Ewan Stewart QC. At the end of the case, the judge, Lord Grant, gave a summing-up considered by many to be highly tendentious, in which he appeared to favour the prosecution. Meehan was duly convicted by a majority verdict and sentenced to life imprisonment. Before he went down, Meehan said clearly to the judge, 'I want to say this sir – I'm innocent of this crime and so is Jim Griffiths.' Turning to the jury, he stated, 'You have made a terrible mistake.'

He immediately lodged an appeal, but this was turned down. The effect on Meehan was devastating. By his own admission a career criminal from the Gorbals, he was by no means a violent man, a fact acknowledged even by the police. In the patois of the underworld Meehan was a 'peterman', or safe-cracker. He claimed that he abhorred violence and was horrified that people would now believe he had brutally attacked an elderly couple. In his autobiography, Meehan wrote that the only violence he was ever involved in was throwing stones at the Orange Walks which passed his boyhood home in the Gorbals every July. Meehan had his own, rather fanciful, theory for his predicament: he believed that he had been framed on the instructions of the British Secret Service. In 1963, he had escaped from Nottingham Prison and, while on the run, ended up in communist East Germany. While in that country he was interrogated by the KGB on how to spring Soviet spies from British jails. Meehan believed that the British authorities planned his downfall from that moment on. It is highly unlikely there was even a grain of truth in his assertion, and the theory has never been given credence by anyone connected to his defence.

In Peterhead Prison, Meehan determined to prove his innocence. As a protest against the conviction, he refused to co-operate with the prison authorities and in 1970 was placed in solitary confinement, where he would remain until his release six years later. It was one of longest periods of solitary confinement in British penal history. At first he conducted his campaign without much assistance from anyone. Meehan was a relentless, persistent and determined advocate of his own cause. He wrote hundreds of letters to people he believed could help him win his freedom. He became an assiduous student of the law of Scotland and even attempted to initiate a private prosecution for perjury against the police officers who had given evidence at the trial.

Gradually people began to listen to his protestations of innocence. They included the BBC journalists David Scott and Ken Vass, and the MPs Frank McElhone and Winnie Ewing. There was also intense interest from the written press: the *Sunday Times*, at that time a crusading newspaper with a reputation for investigative journalism, took up Meehan's case. The eminent author and broadcaster Ludovic Kennedy also became involved and was instrumental in setting up the Free Paddy Meehan Committee in 1972. Kennedy was installed as chairman of the committee and his presence guaranteed that the campaign to free Meehan would remain very much in the public eye.

However, famous and influential names would not be enough to free Meehan. The Scottish legal and political establishments were notoriously reluctant to admit mistakes. This was also a time when the police were considered incorruptible by the press and public. That perception would, of course, be rudely shattered in the 1980s by high-profile miscarriages of justice, such as the cases of the Birmingham Six and the Guildford Four.

Two major developments were to give the campaign a major boost. In a dramatic turn of events, Ian Waddell, who had been impeached by Meehan, confessed to the murder of Rachel Ross, initially to Beltrami, and then in a series of interviews with David Scott, who was wearing a concealed microphone. Waddell also made it unequivocally clear that Meehan was completely innocent of any involvement in the Ross affair, and even offered to give his version of events while under the influence of a so-called 'truth' drug. He then attempted to sell his story to the newspapers for £30,000 but was unable to find a buyer. In July 1973, a television programme with details of Waddell's confession was broadcast on BBC Scotland. An appeal was lodged with Gordon Campbell, the Conservative Secretary of State for Scotland, for the Royal Prerogative of Mercy to be invoked. However, despite the evidence from Waddell, Campbell refused to act.

The second development was equally unexpected. On 25 March 1976 the notorious Glasgow criminal William 'Tank' McGuinness was murdered in a street brawl. The significance was that McGuinness had told Beltrami several years earlier that he was Ian Waddell's accomplice in the robbery and murder at Blackburn Place. He had also, like Waddell, made it clear that Meehan was innocent of these crimes. However, Beltrami, bound by client confidentiality, was unable to make the information public. With the death of McGuinness, he could now use the confession. At last the tide was turning in Meehan's favour.

Free at last! Paddy Meehan and family after his release from prison

The pressure on the authorities was now irresistible. On 19 May 1976 Bruce Millan, the Labour Secretary of State for Scotland, announced in the House of Commons that he would recommend 'the exercise of the Royal Prerogative to grant a Free Pardon'. Patrick Meehan was released the same day. He was understandably embittered: his first words to the waiting world were: 'I want revenge: revenge on the people who put me behind bars.' Nevertheless he was quickly reunited with his wife Betty, who had loyally stood by him throughout his long ordeal. Following a slap-up dinner of T-Bone steak and all the trimmings, Meehan followed another time-honoured tradition, in selling his story to the newspapers. There was, of course, massive media interest, and he quickly made a deal with the *Daily Record*. The fee for his exclusive story was £2,000 and the paper carried extensive extracts for several days. A number of books were later published on the case, including accounts by Ludovic Kennedy, Joe Beltrami and two books from Meehan himself. He later cashed in on his notoriety by co-authoring a book on famous miscarriages of justice.

Although this was the end of Meehan's long ordeal it was by no means the end of the affair. Ian Waddell later stood trial for the murder of Rachel Ross. However, as the only real evidence against him was his own confessions, the jury returned a not-guilty verdict. His trial brought out one more quite amazing fact. On the day of the break-in, 'Tank' McGuinness had been stopped and interviewed by police in Racecourse Road soon after leaving the Rosses' bungalow. McGuinness concocted a cock-and-bull story, and the police gave him a lift to Ayr bus station!

There was also an independent inquiry into the whole affair, chaired by the Scottish judge Lord Hunter. This took five years to complete, but many people close to the case found the inquiry's final report very disappointing. At the same time, Meehan sought compensation for his unjust conviction and incarceration. Initially offered only £7,000, he eventually accepted, albeit reluctantly, the sum of £50,500.

The affair had profound implications for all those it touched. Patrick Meehan, a self-confessed career criminal, was imprisoned for seven years for crimes he did not commit. He later moved to Wales, where he died in 1994 at the age of sixty-seven. James Griffiths, also innocent of any involvement in the crime, was killed by police after shooting dead an innocent bystander in a quiet Glasgow pub and wounding many others. The town of Ayr was deeply affected: one of its citizens had been murdered and another was deeply traumatised by the actions of two vicious hoodlums. Yet perhaps the most serious victim was the Scottish legal system's reputation for fairness and probity. One of the most notable aspects of the case was the establishment's continuing refusal to accept that a terrible mistake had been made, despite the clear evidence of a miscarriage of justice.

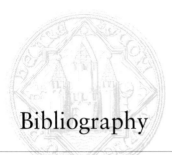

Bibliography

Journals and Periodicals:

Archaeological and Historical Collections of Ayr and Wigton. Ayr and Wigton Archaeological Association, 1878-90

Ayr Advertiser. 1803 to present

Ayrshire Collections, (12 vols). Ayrshire Archaeological and Natural History Society, Ayr, 1947-83

Ayrshire Monographs. Ayrshire Archaeological and Natural History Society, 1987 to present

Ayrshire Notes. Ayrshire Archaeological and Natural History Society and Ayrshire Federation of Historical Societies, 1991 to present

Ayrshire Post. 1880 to present

Scottish Tramlines. Journal of the Scottish Tramway Museum Society, Cambuslang, 1973, 1974

Books:

Anderson, William, *The Scottish Nation.* A. Fullarton, Edinburgh, 1859-63

Anonymous, *Ayrshire – Historical, Commercial & Descriptive.* F.W. Sears, London, 1894

Beltrami, Joseph, *A Deadly Innocence: The Meehan File.* Mainstream, Edinburgh, 1989

Boyle, Andrew M., *The Ayrshire Book of Burns-Lore.* Alloway Publishing, Darvel, 1985

Brash, Ronald W., *The Tramways of Ayr*. NB Traction, Dundee, 1983

Carmichael, Duncan, *The Official History of Ayr United Football Club*. (2 vols) Ayr, 1990, 1992

Davies, Kenneth, *The Clyde Passenger Steamers*. Kyle Publications, Ayr, 1980

Dunlop, Annie I., *The Royal Burgh of Ayr*. Oliver and Boyd, Edinburgh, 1953

Ellis, P. Beresford, and Mac a'Ghobhainn, Seumas, *The Scottish Insurrection of 1820*. Victor Gollancz, London, 1970

Fairbairn, Nicholas, *A Life is Too Short*. Quartet, London, 1987

Fairfax-Blakeborough, John, *Northern Turf History*, Vol. 4. J.A. Allen, London, 1973

Ferguson, James M., *Reminiscences of Auld Ayr*. Ayr Observer, Ayr, 1907

Hamilton of Gilbertfield, William, *Blind Harry's Wallace*. Luath Press, Edinburgh, 1998

Jeffrey, Andrew, *This Time of Crisis*. Mainstream, Edinburgh, 1993

Kennedy, Ludovic, *A Presumption of Innocence*. Victor Gollancz, London, 1975

Leneman, Leah, *A Guid Cause: The Women's Suffrage Movement in Scotland*. Mercat Press, Edinburgh, 1995

Love, Dane, *Pictorial History of Ayr*. Alloway Publishing, Darvel, 1995

   Scottish Covenanter Stories. Neil Wilson Publishing, Glasgow, 2000

Mackenzie, Archibald, *An Ancient Church*. Ayrshire Post, Ayr, 1935

Martin, David J., *Auchincruive*. Scottish Agricultural College, Ayr, 1994

Meehan, Patrick, *Innocent Villain*. Pan Books, London, 1978

Moore, John, *Ayr Gaiety: The Theatre Made Famous by the Popplewells*. Albyn Press, Edinburgh, 1976

Morris, James A., *The Auld Toon o' Ayr*. Stephen and Pollock, Ayr, 1928

Munn, Charles W., *The Scottish Provincial Banking Companies, 1747-1864*. John Donald, Edinburgh, 1981

New Statistical Account of Ayrshire. William Blackwood, Edinburgh, 1842

Paul, J. Balfour, *The Scots Peerage* (9 vols). David Douglas, Edinburgh, 1904-14

Reader, William J., *Macadam: The McAdam Family and the Turnpike Roads 1798-1861*. Heinemann, London, 1980

Robertson, William, *Historical Tales and Legends of Ayrshire*. Hamilton, Adams and Co., London, 1889

Sinclair, Sir John (editor), *The Statistical Account of Scotland*. William Creech, Edinburgh, 1797-9 (21 vols). New edition, Vol. 6, Ayrshire. EP Publishing, Wakefield, 1982

Strawhorn, John, *750 Years of a Scottish School: Ayr Academy 1233-1983*. Alloway Publishing, Ayr, 1983

    The History of Ayr: Royal Burgh and County Town. John Donald, Edinburgh, 1989

Strawhorn, John, and Boyd, William, *The Third Statistical Account of Scotland: Ayrshire*. Oliver and Boyd, Edinburgh, 1951

Tosh, Murray, *Keep Right On . . . The Story of the Conservative Party in the Ayr Burghs and Ayr Constituencies*. Ayr Constituency Conservative Party, 1992

Wilkins, Frances, *Strathclyde's Smuggling Story*. Wyre Forest Press, Kidderminster, 1992

In addition to the above titles, many other pamphlets, guides and maps have been consulted.